"These devotions will give you s
biblical perspective that can tr
—*Adam Robinson, senior pastor of D*
*Birmingham*

D1484564

"*30 Days of Hope for Hurting Marriages* is a tremendous resource
for pastors, ministry leaders, counselors, and other church leaders
and is a must read for every married couple.
We need more books like this one!"
—*Dr. Garry K. Brantley, senior minister of CrossBridge Church,
Birmingham, AL*

"The insights and encouragement provided in *30 Days
of Hope for Hurting Marriages* will prove invaluable to
those who may be struggling."
—*Dr. Mark Searby, director of doctor of ministry studies and director of
student services at Beeson Divinity School*

"*30 Days of Hope for Hurting Marriages* offers godly wisdom,
encouragement, and hope for those in the storm. As a pastoral
counselor, I now have a fresh and powerful resource to
share with hurting couples."
—*Rodney A. Wilson, marriages pastor at LifePoint Church, Smyrna, TN*

"*30 Days of Hope for Hurting Marriages* highlights the hindrances
and embraces the solutions, reveals the problems and offers pos-
sibilities, conveys the obstacles and encourages the opportunities."
—*Dr. Robert Smith Jr., Charles T. Carter Baptist Chair of Divinity,
Beeson Divinity School*

"Putting into practice the things discussed in this book will help
any marriage begin the journey toward wholeness and hope."
—*Brian Lee, senior pastor, Shades Crest Baptist Church, Birmingham, AL*

"This collection of daily devotionals will encourage marriage part-
ners to keep hope alive as they individually open themselves to
God's healing grace. Hope for what may seem hopelessly broken
leaps off the page day after day in this devotional guide."
—*Clella A. Lee, fellow ministry partner throughout
Randy and Melody's marital journey*

GIFTS OF HOPE SERIES

# 30 DAYS OF HOPE
## FOR HURTING MARRIAGES

# RANDY AND MELODY
# HEMPHILL

NEW HOPE®
PUBLISHERS
Gospel-Centered. Missions-Driven.

BIRMINGHAM, ALABAMA

New Hope® Publishers
PO Box 12065
Birmingham, AL 35202-2065
NewHopePublishers.com
New Hope Publishers is a division of WMU®.

Library of Congress Cataloging-in-Publication Data

Names: Hemphill, Randy, 1974- author.
Title: 30 days of hope for hurting marriages / by Randy and Melody Hemphill.
Other titles: Thirty days of hope for hurting marriages
Description: Birmingham, AL : New Hope Publishers, 2016.
Identifiers: LCCN 2016025521 (print) | LCCN 2016027120 (ebook) | ISBN
   9781625915078 (sc) | ISBN 9781596699618 (e-book)
Subjects: LCSH: Marriage--Religious aspects--Christianity.
Classification: LCC BV835 .H456 2016 (print) | LCC BV835 (ebook) | DDC
   248.8/44--dc23
LC record available at https://lccn.loc.gov/2016025521

ISBN-13: 978-1-62591-507-8

N174106 • 1016 • 1M1

*To the many couples who have allowed us to journey with them through the heartache of a hurting marriage. And to our God who is able to do the impossible. May these pages bear witness to the One who restores broken people and broken marriages.*

# TABLE OF CONTENTS

# INTRODUCTION

A ND they lived happily ever after!" Screen darkens. Romantic music swells. Roll the credits.

All of us wish our marriages could end like the movies. The happy couple walking into the sunset holding hands while soft music plays in the background. Picture perfect!

We enter marriage with these love-struck dreams. Swept away in romance, we share vows and life together begins.

But eventually the music stops. For some it fades slowly. The love that once drew husband and wife together seems like a distant, haunting memory. The years of work, children, bills, losses, or simply "trying harder" take a toll on the relationship. And a couple finds themselves in the clutches of despair. With no way out and little desire to get there, he gives in to despair. She throws in the emotional towel. And both settle—or give up. A marriage that is hurting.

For others, the music comes to a dramatic halt. An affair surfaces abruptly. The secret addiction is exposed. Bankruptcy is filed—either financially or emotionally. She says, "I'm just not in love with you." He says, "I'm done." And divorce stares them in the face. Both are devastated, ready to give up. A marriage that is hurting.

Maybe you can connect with some of the heartache. Your circumstances are unique and your feelings are real. You probably picked up this book because something is not right. Whether it is clear or a bit foggy, you know your marriage is hurting. And we also guess that you want to do something about it. Though part of you wants to give in or give up, you picked up this book because you want some hope.

We understand. And we do not say that lightly. We have faced hopeless seasons in our marriage. We have dealt with disappointment, anger, hurt, confusion, and fear. We have been on the edge of divorce. We have experienced and been eyewitnesses to restoration in dark times. And we believe there is hope for hurting marriages. We really do believe!

We promise a few things in this journey . . .

WE WILL VALIDATE YOUR FEELINGS. Instead of offering up simple fixes or nice and tidy to-do lists, we want to validate your pain, anger, or fears. What you feel matters and your pain is real. We hope that you have several "So, I'm not alone" moments in these pages. Though feelings are not the right foundation for making decisions, we do want to validate your emotions.

WE WILL SPEAK THE TRUTH. We do not want to leave you alone in the heartache or hopelessness. Instead of offering up self-help strategies or secular wisdom, we rely on the truths of God's Word to guide the journey. Our marriages need to be grounded in the principles and wisdom provided by God so that we can reflect His character and heart. We commit to speaking God's truth to your situation.

WE WILL FIGHT FOR YOUR MARRIAGE. You are not alone. Times of testing in marriage can lead you to feel like you have to walk on your own. You probably feel like you are the only one fighting for something more in your relationship. We pray that you are encouraged through these devotions and that God will strengthen you in this season of weakness. Let's fight together for your marriage. Be encouraged. Your marriage is worth it!

There are two ways to begin this book of devotions. You can begin with Day 1, or you can go to the section that best describes your present emotional state. No matter where you begin, we pray that you will find hope today. We pray that you discover the Creator and Restorer of relationships—God Himself. And we pray that your marriage experiences healing in the days to come.

To that end,
*Randy and Melody*

# MEET THE AUTHORS

R ANDY and Melody's story is one filled with brokenness and healing.

Married in June of 1995, their individual stories became one, though neither realized the wounds and struggles each brought into their marriage. It would be several years before their emotional and spiritual challenges surfaced. In 2003, their marriage collapsed after Melody's affair was exposed. Randy's internal struggles with passivity, insecurity, and depression came to light. The future looked bleak and restoration felt impossible.

Only the love of Jesus could rescue them from the sinful, broken choices they made. God exposed, pursued, and began to slowly restore them, both individually and together. What seemed impossible, God made possible through a process of restoration in each of them that led to the healing of their marriage.

*Brokenness* and *restoration* are not seasonal terms for Randy and Melody. These practices are vital to a daily walk with God. A call to dependency on God keeps them fighting for their marriage and the marriages of others. They were led to start LIFE Ministries with a vision to build up the local church by building healthy marriages. Through teaching, writing, and counseling, they have spent the last several years ministering to men, women, and couples.

They have been blessed with four children and a relationship marked by honesty and vulnerability. Both of them have degrees from Campbell University. Randy has graduate degrees from Beeson Divinity School of Samford University. His doctor of ministry specialized in the pastoral practice of spiritual direction. To learn more, visit lifeministriesnow.com.

# I MARRIED THE WRONG PERSON

*I'm not trying to get my way in the world's way.*
*I'm trying to get your way, your Word's way.*
*I'm staying on your trail; I'm putting one foot in front*
*of the other. I'm not giving up.*

—PSALM 17:4–5 THE MESSAGE

**RELATIONSHIP TOXIN:** I married the wrong person.

**RELATIONSHIP PRACTICE:** Staying put

C AN we have an honest conversation today about marriage?

Has the question, "Did I marry the wrong person?" ever crossed your mind? Maybe the question hit you after a disagreement or fight. Or it may be consuming your thoughts on the heels of a lengthy season of pain and weariness.

In the monotony of doing life together, our minds begin to wander. This question gets nestled in our thoughts, typically prompted by unmet expectations. The life you and I believed we would have is not quite measuring up.

When Melody and I went through the near-loss of our marriage, it made us question everything. Maybe we married the wrong people. We thought there was another life out there with someone who might appreciate us, value us, and usher in happiness. In our early days and months of recovery, we chose to make decisions based on what was right versus what we felt. We wanted to give the relationship a chance and not dictate possible outcomes based on our emotions. Although, we must express our feelings in order to be emotionally healthy, catering to our emotions is not the best way to make wise decisions— especially long-term decisions.

In the marriage journey, there are disciplines or practices that we need to implement because they help draw us close to one another and to God. The point is not necessarily the discipline itself, but the intended result of deeper intimacy.

One of the ways to cure our souls of this particular marriage toxin (*I married the wrong person*) is to practice the discipline of staying put. Our marriages need staying power and the stick-to-it kind of commitment that a deeper life with God can bring.

Let us first clarify what the discipline of staying put does not mean. It does not mean giving up, settling for a mediocre marriage, or being strangers in the same house. Staying put does not mean allowing any form of abuse. It does not mean turning a blind eye to the glaring issues in your marriage. Staying put does not equal complacency, apathy, or putting your head in the sand. Instead of throwing in the towel, this spiritual practice enables us to dig our heels in and take up the towel of Christlike service.

Here is what staying put means. It means dealing with self. It means that instead of living in denial, you choose to deal with the glaring relational issues in your own life. Why do you avoid conflict, seek to control, struggle to listen, berate others, inflate others, beat yourself up, prop yourself up, etc.? Instead of running or pointing the finger at someone else, when you stay put, you choose to look firmly in the mirror and deal with the person you see staring back at you. Instead of seeing your spouse as a barrier to grace, you choose to view marriage as a sacrament, a vehicle of God's grace.

The discipline of staying put forces us to look at the issues in our marriages and engage in a process of healing and freedom.

Only in relationships that encourage no bailing out can certain levels of growth take place. This is why traditional marriage vows emphasize for better, for worse and 'til death do us part. These are ways of saying "I promise to stay put."

Husbands: will you choose to stay put? Wives: will you choose to stay put?

To combat negative thoughts in marriage, apply 2 Corinthians 10:5, "We demolish arguments and every pretension that sets itself up against the knowledge of God, and we take captive every thought to make it obedient to Christ." Write down and admit to God any negative thoughts that you are having about your spouse or marriage. To the side of those thoughts, in a separate column, write down a truth to combat each negative thought and to give you staying power today.

## REFLECTIONS

◉ Why is the question, "Did I marry the wrong person?" toxic to your marriage?

◉ How are you letting feelings of confusion or despair rule your day or control your mind?

◉ Why is staying put such an important spiritual practice in marriage?

◉ What is one thing you can do today to honor your commitment to stay put?

# WHY DID GOD LET THIS HAPPEN?

*Therefore, in order to keep me from becoming
conceited, I was given a thorn in my flesh,
a messenger of Satan, to torment me. Three times
I pleaded with the Lord to take it away from me.
But he said to me, "My grace is sufficient for you,
for my power is made perfect in weakness."
Therefore I will boast all the more gladly about my
weaknesses, so that Christ's power may rest on me.
That is why, for Christ's sake, I delight in weaknesses,
in insults, in hardships, in persecutions, in difficulties.
For when I am weak, then I am strong.*

—2 Corinthians 12:7–10

CINDY felt scattered as she looked for the TV remote. It always seemed like this little device had the ability to grow legs and play hide-and-seek. She drifted off to the bedroom to catch a break and a much needed mental rest. Her frustration over the lost remote paled in comparison to the despair and confusion that stifled her heart.

With the noise of kids playing in the family room, she shut the bedroom door and began the search. She just wanted a breather, an escape for a few minutes. As she knelt down and pulled up the bed skirt, she saw the remote perched up against a box. She dragged the box out, wiped off the dust, and realized that it was their wedding album.

The memories flooded her mind. *How could we have drifted so far in such a short amount of time?* Tears ran down her cheeks and onto her hand, pressed against the photo album. She cried out in pain, "God, why . . . why . . . why did you let this happen?"

Cindy's story, though hypothetical, is common in marriage.

Where is God when life gets messy?

Where is God when marriage feels hopeless?

Most of us experience chapters in our marriage that we wish could be edited out. It could be that you are moving through one of those chapters right now. Despair replaces dreams. And more questions fill the air than answers.

Paul had some questions. He prayed for God to remove something from his life . . . he called it a "thorn in the flesh" (2 Corinthians 12:7–10). He says that he prayed three times for God to remove it. Paul was asking the same question Cindy asked, "God, why did you allow this to happen?" Though the nature of Paul's thorn is uncertain, we do know that it was painful, confusing, and gut-wrenching.

And God's answer? "My grace is sufficient for you, for my power is made perfect in weakness" (v. 9). In other words, "Paul, I know this situation is painful. I know you would like Me to remove it. Instead of pulling you out of this, I am going to enter into it with you. I am going to deliver strength and grace in your weakness. Trust Me."

Thorns are perplexing. They are situations or circumstances that can be used by the enemy, Satan, to defeat us and deplete us. They can lure us away from God, leading to confusion and mistrust. And thorns can also be fertile ground for grace. Paul stayed put in the thorny situation so that God's power might rest on him. God does not need you to fix the marriage or to fix yourself. He knows you cannot. Instead, He is asking you to trust Him today. Trust Him with your fears. Trust Him with your confusion. Trust Him with your tears and your anger. Trust Him with the "Why?" Let His power and grace rest on you today.

## REFLECTIONS

- What is the thorn you are struggling with today?

- How might the enemy, Satan, wish to use this thorn to lure you into doubt, fear, and mistrust of God?

- How might God, as Father, want to use this thorn to deliver His grace and strength in your life?

- Write out an honest prayer detailing your struggles and questions along with your trust in Him. Write 2 Corinthians 12:7–10 on a note card and carry it with you today.

DAY 3

# DECISIONS, DECISIONS, DECISIONS

*I will instruct you and teach you in the way*
*you should go; I will counsel you with my loving eye*
*on you. Do not be like the horse or mule,*
*which have no understanding but must be controlled*
*by bit and bridle or they will not come to you.*
*Many are the woes of the wicked, but the LORD's*
*unfailing love surrounds the one who trusts in him.*
*Rejoice in the LORD and be glad, you righteous;*
*sing, all you who are upright in heart.*

—PSALM 32:8–11

W<small>E</small> have counseled many couples over the years in crisis situations. When crisis hits, there is normally a pressure to decide what to do. Sometimes friends and family are the first to offer opinions about the decisions you should make. Well-intentioned but biased allies can muddy the waters when you are trying to make clear and wise choices.

You may be wondering . . .

*Should we separate?*
*Is it too late?*
*What about the kids?*
*Will he ever get over this?*
*Will my spouse trust me again?*
*Will she ever say she's sorry?*
*What's next?*

And the list goes on and on. So many decisions knocking at the door of your heart and your marriage. How do you typically handle them? You are probably either a pusher or a procrastinator.

**DECISION-PUSHERS.** Pushers struggle with indecision and the unknown. They want to arrive at a choice and move on. When things go south in a marriage, pushers are the first to draw conclusions and make plans for next steps. On one hand, there is strength in this mind-set. You are probably a get-it-done type of person. You see the reality of the relationship and push for resolution. You play a vital role in setting up counseling, pressing for communication, or dealing with glaring issues in a marriage. On the other hand, your impatience can lead to quick decisions and forced steps. If you act too quickly or directly, your spouse may push back and harbor resentment against you.

**DECISION-PROCRASTINATORS.** Procrastinators can sometimes come across as lazy, but they tend to be processors. It takes time for them to work through feelings and options. On one hand, processors help slow things down. You realize that the marriage is spiraling or hurting. You may even see that divorce is knocking at the door. You are helpful in creating a "pause" that allows emotions to settle before making a life-changing decision. On the other hand, this slowdown can lead to procrastination, denial, or laziness in moving forward. If you delay too long, you may come across as apathetic or uncaring.

What is a healthy approach to decision-making at this stage of your marriage?

Reread the Scripture for today. Whenever you read the word *you* or *the one*, replace it with your name. Personalize this psalm, and draw strength from it today as you work toward decisions. Here are three truths from this psalm:

LET GOD FATHER YOU. This psalm reminds us that God, as a loving father, will instruct, teach, and counsel us in times of decision. His "loving eye" is on you during this time of confusion, doubt, and decision-making. Instead of imposing or forcing a choice, let God provide counsel on the next steps in your process. Don't live in denial or wait to ask God for help. Instead, let God instruct and father you in the healing of your heart and your marriage.

FIGHT THE TENDENCY TO CONTROL, WITH VULNERABILITY. Psalm 32 talks about a horse or mule that needs to be led or controlled by bit and bridle. The image is that of someone who fights being led and must be controlled or pulled along. In a relationship with God, control suffocates our intimacy with

Him. It also stifles openness with our spouse. We fight our controlling tendencies by practicing vulnerability and exerting faith in God. Vulnerability leads us to admit our brokenness to God and our dependency on Him for healing and restoration. Choose today to fight the tendency to control with a vulnerable, open heart.

TRUST GOD TODAY. Psalm 32 ends with the truth that God's unfailing love surrounds those who trust in Him. We can rejoice and sing, even in the darkest of circumstances, because our trust is in the unwavering love of God. He is in control. He is able to redeem and use the weakness of our stories. He is able to heal the most broken marriage. Trust Him today.

## REFLECTIONS

- List the major decisions you are facing. Writing out the decisions will help you in praying and releasing them to God.

- What fears do you have about being vulnerable with God and others?

- Name a few ways that you try to take control in relationships.

- Make a concerted effort to trust God today and lean on Him for the decisions you are facing.

# IN A FOG

*Again Jesus spoke to them, saying,*
*"I am the light of the world.*
*Whoever follows me will not walk in darkness,*
*but will have the light of life."*

—JOHN 8:12 ESV

**RELATIONSHIP TOXIN:** Letting the confusing fog of my circumstances dictate my decisions

**RELATIONSHIP PRACTICE:** Pursuing truth while in the fog

FOG. It is thick and it obscures our view. It is dark. It makes seeing what is ahead impossible. Fog muddles reality for us. Fog leaves us longing for clarity, yet reminds us that we cannot see. We cannot make sense of what is behind us, and we cannot see anything before us except for the dense clouds. Oh, how fog can keep us in a place of confusion and despair. I (Melody) have lived it and felt consumed by it. I have been completely paralyzed by it.

When our marriage was at its lowest point, I remember waking up each day feeling like I could not think a clear thought. There would be a few moments each morning, before I remembered the state of my life, where the day seemed like any other day. But, how quickly that changed when reality came crashing down on me and I realized that I had no idea what the day would hold, what the future held, and the fog settled in quickly and thickly around my mind and heart. I felt stuck, unable to make sense of my choices, my unhealthy ways of coping, and my sins. And the only thing in front of me was cloudy confusion mixed with some hopelessness and despair. The fog overcame me. My mind was filled with questions such as, "How do I pray?" "How do I hope?" and "How do I trust?"

One of the Satan's greatest methods of attack on us—when our own sins or the sins of our spouses bring heartbreak to our marriages—is to make reaching out to God feel impossible. If he can convince us that the fog is real and immovable, then we will be unable to believe and live in God's truth. The enemy's lies surround us and permeate our thoughts—his lies that God is not here, our marriage will not recover, and that the fog is an indication of how the rest of our lives will be. Satan uses confusion to keep us from truth.

In our Scripture for today, Jesus says that He is the light of the world and His followers will have the light of life. This stands in contrast to walking in darkness and living in a fog. The light of Jesus can break through our fog and allow us to see clearly and make healthy decisions.

Believers in Jesus Christ know that confusion is not from God. First Corinthians 14:33 (NJKV) tells us, "God is not the author of confusion, but of peace." Friend, the fog you are in is a tool of the enemy to make you feel stuck and afraid. And God's Word clearly tells us that any confusion we currently feel is not from Him. He is the author of peace. And the truth of His love, mercy, and grace are the very beliefs we must hold to when the fog is thick and we cannot see what is on the horizon.

God is sovereign. He sees beyond our fog and desperately wants to lead us to the other side of it. He knows what will happen next in our marriage, with our family, with our future. If we will take His hand in the middle of our darkness, He will walk us through it until we are able to see clearly again. He is a good Father. God doesn't want His sons and daughters to walk alone blindly. As we would take the hands of our own children to lead them to safety, God desires to do the same for us. Our responsibility is to reach out for help. We must admit our great need, the darkness and confusion that surround us, and our willingness to let God lead as only He can do. He will be faithful to lead us beyond the fog into days of greater awareness of our brokenness, deeper dependence on Him, and a clear view ahead where He is leading us each step of the way.

## REFLECTIONS

⊚Do you feel as though you are in a fog due to the current circumstances of your marriage?

⊚How is the fog affecting your ability to see God in the midst of your situation?

⊚Do you believe God can and will lead you to thinking clear and true thoughts?

⊚What is the next step for you to take toward a greater dependence on Christ, which will protect you from the lies of the enemy?

## DAY 5

# WHAT'S WRONG
# WITH ME?

*When I heard this, I sat down and wept.*
*I mourned for days, fasting and praying*
*before the God-of-Heaven. I said, "GOD,*
*God-of-Heaven, the great and awesome God,*
*loyal to his covenant and faithful to those*
*who love him and obey his commands:*
*Look at me, listen to me. Pay attention to this prayer*
*of your servant that I'm praying day and night*
*in intercession for your servants, the People of Israel,*
*confessing the sins of the People of Israel.*
*And I'm including myself, I and my ancestors,*
*among those who have sinned against you.*

*We've treated you like dirt: We haven't done what you told us, haven't followed your commands, and haven't respected the decisions you gave to Moses your servant. All the same, remember the warning you posted to your servant Moses: 'If you betray me, I'll scatter you to the four winds, but if you come back to me and do what I tell you, I'll gather up all these scattered peoples from wherever they ended up and put them back in the place I chose to mark with my Name.'"*

—Nehemiah 1:4–9 The Message

---

WHAT do you do when the walls of your marriage have collapsed?

I (Randy) remember *the* night like it was yesterday. After things exploded in our marriage, I packed some bags and left to stay at a friend's house during our separation. At the time, I thought we were done. Trust vanished and hope seemed beyond reach. I began to wonder in my confusion, "What's wrong with me?"

This question showed up in a variety of ways.

What's wrong with me? Am I not enough? Marital struggles cut close to the heart and are always personal. If your spouse has an affair or secret addiction, you feel disregarded, as if your spouse has chosen another over you, leaving you to wonder why the marriage was not enough. If romance has faded from lack of attention or affection, you might be confused as to how the flames of passion have been extinguished. If anger or confusion has set in because of unmet needs or hurtful words, you probably feel at a loss for next steps. Each of these causes a person to question his or her self-worth and the future of marriage.

What's wrong with me? How did I make such pitiful choices? If you have betrayed the trust in your marriage, you are looking back trying to make sense of your decisions. If you have been betrayed, you are questioning your trust and belief in the relationship. The truth is we all make bad decisions that carry consequences throughout our lives. Confusing seasons of marriage cause you to look back and second-guess your choices.

What's wrong with me? Will I ever trust again? Questioning yourself leads to uncertainty about the restoration of your relationship. So many thoughts about being able to move forward run through your mind. You might be wondering if you can trust God. You might be wondering whether you can trust your spouse again. So much confusion surrounds with an equal number of questions.

Nehemiah faced a similar situation when he realized that the walls of Jerusalem had been destroyed. It was a sad and confusing time for God's people. Over the years, the walls that represented safety and trust crumbled. Enemies conquered the nation of Israel and carried most of its people into captivity. Walls, historically speaking, were a significant symbol of protection and trust. For the walls to be broken down meant that confusion and fear filled the people's hearts.

Nehemiah's response to the news can inform the way we behave today in our marriages. Initially, he responded with deep sadness and weeping. He was overcome with emotion at the loss and devastation. Instead of hiding his grief, he expressed it openly and honestly. This led to a prayer that we find in Nehemiah 1.

Here is what we learn from his prayer:

OWN YOUR STUFF. Nehemiah could have allowed his grief to breed blame and anger toward the people and their choices. And he would probably have been "right" in doing so. On the other hand, Nehemiah could have allowed his grief and confusion to spawn self-blame or self-hatred. Instead, Nehemiah included himself in the confessional prayer. He said, *we* have committed sins against God and *we* have treated God like dirt. He owned his own sin while also confessing the sins of the people. Your marriage (singular) is your marriage (plural). The path forward involves confession of your own mistakes and failures along with the brokenness of your marriage as a whole. Instead of blame, choose to pray with honesty and ownership.

RELEASE YOUR SPOUSE TO GOD. While Nehemiah prayed for God's people, he also released them to make a choice in how they would move forward. Though he would speak on their behalf and lay out a restoration plan, the choice was theirs. It could not be forced or coerced. You can pray for your spouse and for your marriage. You can fight—and you ought to—for restoration. But you also have to release your spouse to God and to his or her own choices.

COMMIT TO A PROCESS. After approaching the king for permission to go to Jerusalem in chapter 2, Nehemiah begins the process of rebuilding the walls. It involved every person's gifts and skills. It required great effort on behalf of the whole community. But with God's help, the walls were rebuilt in a relatively short amount of time. *Process* is the key word for you. It is not a choice to "fix" your spouse or "fix" your marriage. It involves a commitment to a process. In the midst of your confusion and "What's wrong with me?" questions, will you choose a process of rebuilding the walls of your marriage?

## REFLECTIONS

◉ Are you taking time to examine your own heart— to ask God to bring issues to light that you need to work on?

◉ How are the walls down in your marriage?

◉ What does it mean to own your stuff while also releasing your spouse to God?

◉ What is the next step in your process that could potentially rebuild the walls of your marriage?

# THINKING
# CLEARLY

*For the word of God is alive and active.*
*Sharper than any double-edged sword,*
*it penetrates even to dividing soul and spirit,*
*joints and marrow; it judges the thoughts*
*and attitudes of the heart.*

—Hebrews 4:12

D o you feel as if your mind will never be clear again? Does it seem like confusion and fog have settled in for the long haul and will never leave? If you feel that way, I (Melody) can relate. I have been there, struggling to make sense of my life and my circumstances, and feeling like my thoughts were so conflicting that I did not know which way was up. I have walked through seasons in our marriage in which I experienced two opposite emotions and had two opposite desires simultaneously. I honestly thought I was losing my mind trying to sort through an onslaught of thoughts and feelings I did not know how to reconcile. It made me feel crazy at best and hopeless at worst. Our thoughts are powerful and can take us to a place of greater dependence on Christ or into an unhealthy cycle of mental and emotional confusion and frustration.

I want to offer you some hope today. After a lengthy season of a crumbling marriage and a destructive personal life, God did restore my mind. I spent a long time pursuing my fleshly desires, and it led to a time where our marriage seemed lost forever. As I made different choices, which greatly impacted the future of my marriage, I realized that healing and restoration starts with your thoughts.

Romans 8:5–6 (ESV) described my life:

> For those who live according to the flesh set their minds on the things of the flesh, but those who live according to the Spirit set their minds on the things of the Spirit. For to set the mind on the flesh is death, but to set the mind on the Spirit is life and peace.

I had set my mind on things of the flesh, and it was leading to my own spiritual death and ultimately the death of my marriage.

When God brought my destructive patterns to light, I had a choice to make. I could either continue to set my mind on what I thought I wanted, or I could set my mind on the things of God. I ultimately desired real life and peace, but I had been looking in all of the wrong places to get it.

As I began to seek God's desires for my life and marriage, 2 Corinthians 10:5 (ESV) became my daily prayer, "We destroy arguments and every lofty opinion raised against the knowledge of God, and take every thought captive to obey Christ." I wrote that verse on note cards and placed them on my bathroom mirror, the dashboard of my car, and my refrigerator. My fleshly thoughts controlled my life for a long time, and nothing good had come from it. I knew in my heart that my freedom and healing would only come when my thoughts were taken captive to be obedient to Christ. My disobedience had brought so much pain to so many people. I realized that being in charge of my own thoughts was not working. Only thoughts that died to my flesh and led me to a life of obedience to Christ would bring about the life and relationships that I longed for.

As I surrendered my thoughts to God, asking Him to change them, remove them, clarify them, and heal them as He saw fit, I began to experience freedom that was missing in my life for a very long time. I began to think clearly again. I was able to hear God's voice of discernment over my life and choices, and my thoughts, emotions, and actions began to line up with what I believed were God's next steps for me. Though intentional, it was not easy. God was faithful to take all my surrendered thoughts, whether crazy, irrational, selfish, or hurtful, and bring them under His authority. It did bring peace. It did bring life. It did bring restoration. Because He did it for me, I believe with all of my heart that He will do it for you.

# REFLECTIONS

⊚ How are your thoughts affecting you during this confusing season of marriage?

⊚ Write out the thoughts that need to be taken captive by Christ and placed under His authority.

⊚ Are you willing to take your thoughts to Him, moment by moment, in order to find healing and freedom? Why or why not?

# ANGER IS LOVE DISAPPOINTED

*"Will the Lord reject forever? Will he never show his favor again? Has his unfailing love vanished forever? Has his promise failed for all time? Has God forgotten to be merciful? Has he in anger withheld his compassion?" Then I thought, "To this I will appeal: the years when the Most High stretched out his right hand. I will remember the deeds of the LORD; yes, I will remember your miracles of long ago. I will consider all your works and meditate on all your mighty deeds." Your ways, God, are holy. What god is as great as our God? You are the God who performs miracles; you display your power among the peoples.*

*—PSALM 77:7–14*

T HERE's a line from an old Eagles song that goes like this, "They say that anger is just love disappointed." Pretty true, isn't it? Marriage . . . love . . . disappointment . . . they seem to go together.

Maybe you can connect with some of these phrases . . .

*I'm just tired of trying.*
*Why does this have to be so hard?*
*We keep having the same conversation over and over and over.*
*I don't know if he'll ever change.*
*She just won't listen to me.*
*Maybe this is as good as it gets.*

Disappointment . . . ugh! It takes the wind out of your sails and gives you a sinking feeling.

Several years ago, Melody and I were going through the most trying time of our marriage. Divorce was more than knocking at the door, it was sitting at our kitchen table. Both of us felt like there was no way out. And I remember feeling extremely disappointed with myself and with us. Call it frustration. The truth is, I was angry.

## ANGRY AND DISAPPOINTED WITH MYSELF

There are times when our anger turns inward, toward ourselves. Maybe you were the primary person who caused the decline in your marriage and shame keeps hanging around. Maybe you were betrayed and are angry that you let yourself be taken advantage of. We can suppress or depress our anger, which suffocates the heart, or we can project it on others, which pushes people away. At the core, we are angry with ourselves.

## ANGRY AND DISAPPOINTED WITH MY SPOUSE

To love is to experience disappointment. The only way to avoid disappointment is to shut your heart off from experiencing love. We must take the risk to love, which opens us up to disappointment. You might be frustrated with your spouse for working too much or too little, talking too much or too little, neglecting the marriage, or simply checking out. If that's the case, your anger is creating distance and emotional separation. Or maybe you are downright mad at your spouse. A betrayal, secret, or lie has blindsided your relationship, leaving you hurt and angry. If that's the case, it is hard to imagine being able to love him or her again.

## ANGRY AND DISAPPOINTED WITH GOD

All of this anger and disappointment spills over into our relationship with God. How could God let this happen? Does He care? Will He come through for me? We tend to feel guilty about expressing anger to God, so we mask it with religious efforts, trying harder. Or we simply pull away. Disappointment with God, even doubts, are normal. But if our anger is left unexpressed or unhealed, it leads to resentment and disconnection.

What do I do with my anger and disappointments? Here are a few steps:

EXPLORE THE WAYS YOU DEAL WITH ANGER. Everyone has a story of anger. How did your father and mother deal with anger? Was anger a safe emotion in your home? When did you first experience a major disappointment of love in a relationship? How have you handled your anger over the years? How would others say that you handle your anger?

EXPRESS WITHOUT TRYING TO FIX. Anger is not a good or bad emotion. It is an emotion that can lead to constructive or destructive behaviors. The healthy path in a relationship is emotional honesty. We must express our anger without trying to fix or point a finger at someone. We often talk with couples about using "I" statements instead of "You always" or "You never" statements. Own your anger with your spouse or with God and express it honestly.

TAKE YOUR ANGER AND DISAPPOINTMENT TO GOD. HE WILL LISTEN AND FATHER YOU. Instead of masking your anger, take it to God. He wants to hear from you. The Book of Psalms is a great place to begin. David, who authored many psalms, boldly expresses his anger with God and others. He vents instead of suppressing. He communicates instead of attacking. And David always comes back to trust and faith. It might help to create a prayer journal in which you can express your anger and write out your prayers.

## REFLECTIONS

⊚ What are the first three to five words that come to mind when you think of anger?

⊚ How did you learn to express or suppress anger growing up?

⊚ What are you currently disappointed or angry about? How would others say that you are dealing with the anger?

⊚ Write freely about the frustrations with which you are currently wrestling. Take those words and formulate them into a prayer to God.

# YOUR SPOUSE IS NOT THE ENEMY

*Therefore, having put away falsehood,*
*let each one of you speak the truth with his neighbor,*
*for we are members one of another.*
*Be angry and do not sin;*
*do not let the sun go down on your anger,*
*and give no opportunity to the devil.*

—Ephesians 4:25–27 ESV

B ILL was rummaging through an old desk drawer when he came across a picture from high school. He and Linda had fallen in love during their sophomore year. This picture was from the spring dance. Bill chuckled as he remembered the tuxedo he rented with the matching bow tie and cummerbund combo. Both were navy blue to match the gown Linda wore that evening. The picture reminded him of their smiles and sense of innocence that seemed like a lifetime ago.

As he stared at the old photo, he wondered how he had become so angry over the years. The smile had faded and been replaced with a frown of resentment. The innocence that once characterized their love had been jaded by mistrust and pain. Oh, how he longed to have that relationship back. And he knew that Linda had those same desires. But, it seemed impossible. The anger ran so deep for both of them. It was as if a giant, emotional wall had been built up over the years, one brick at a time.

Anger, if buried or misdirected, can have a destructive effect on a relationship. If we bury it, it grows like a cancer inside, destroying love and vulnerability. If misdirected, our words lash out and form deep trenches of resentment. One of the most fatal blows that comes from unhealthy anger is that we begin to view our spouse as the enemy.

What a strategic move by the true enemy, Satan! In order to take the spotlight off his evil plan, he convinces us that our spouse is actually the source of all pain and loss. Shining the light on her husband, a wife can become resentful about unmet needs and past hurts. Persuading a husband that his wife is the enemy, Satan leads a man down the road of a cold shoulder and isolated heart. A marriage grows stale and can even fall apart when a husband and wife view each other as the enemy.

We certainly do not want to downplay the anger and hurt you are experiencing. More than likely, your spouse has let you down a lot. Much of your anger is appropriate as it matches the depth of your love. To love is to risk being hurt. Anger is a normal response to hurt. It is normal to experience bouts of anger in a marriage. The key is what we *do* with our anger.

Anger is a great, God-given emotion. Some of us have a purely negative view of anger. We see it as a solely destructive emotion. But the truth is anger can actually be used to grow relationships.

Here are a few truths about anger from Ephesians 4.

EXPRESS ANGER HONESTLY WITH YOUR SPOUSE (EPHESIANS 4:25). It's dishonest to hide your anger. Your spouse needs to know about the hurts and resentment you carry. An honest conversation can be frightening to some. You might fear losing the relationship or being rejected. You might fear being misunderstood if you share your anger in honesty. In reality, if you do not share, the relationship may continue to be suffocated by your bitterness. The only way to clear the air and take steps forward is to be honest with your anger.

EXPRESS ANGER OPENLY (EPHESIANS 4:26). This next verse has two truths for marriage. The first is to be angry without sinning or hurting the other person. We tell our clients to use "I" statements. Attacking your spouse with anger and pointing out all of the ways that he or she is not measuring up will automatically put him or her on the defensive. Instead of hearing you, your spouse will be planning his or her closing argument. Share your anger openly, honestly, and personally. An example of such a statement might be, "I feel hurt when you do not listen to me," or "I don't feel considered when you put work or the kids before us." The second truth from this verse: do not let the sun go down on our anger. Don't let it fester into resentment and bitterness. The verse does not necessarily mean that anger has to be settled before the calendar switches to the next day. There are times when sleeping on it allows for emotions to settle, for a more productive conversation later on. The truth is to express anger in a timely manner. The longer that anger brews inside, the more likely it is to become destructive.

EXPRESS ANGER TOWARD YOUR TRUE ENEMY (EPHESIANS 4:27). We give the devil opportunity when we treat our spouse like the enemy. To dismiss the enemy's role in relational struggles is to rule out a primary character in the story. Your story has a villain and his name is Satan. His desire is to destroy followers of Jesus Christ and take their marriages down too. When a marriage is destroyed, the ripple effect of evil is great. Share your anger honestly and appropriately with your spouse and remember that your spouse is not your enemy. Funnel your anger toward the devil as a way of fighting for your marriage.

## REFLECTIONS

⊚ How have you sometimes viewed your spouse as the enemy?

⊚ How might it affect your marriage if both of you shared anger honestly while viewing Satan as your enemy?

⊚ What is one thing you need to share with your spouse today?

⊚ Rewrite Ephesians 4:25–27 in your own words, and personalize the verses.

# DON'T BURY IT

*Come quickly, LORD, and answer me,*
*for my depression deepens. Don't turn away from me,*
*or I will die. Let me hear of your unfailing love*
*each morning, for I am trusting you.*
*Show me where to walk, for I give myself to you.*
*Rescue me from my enemies, LORD;*
*I run to you to hide me. Teach me to do your will,*
*for you are my God. May your gracious Spirit*
*lead me forward on a firm footing.*
*For the glory of your name, O LORD, preserve my life.*
*Because of your faithfulness,*
*bring me out of this distress.*

—PSALM 143:7–11 NLT

I (RANDY) have struggled with depression intermittently throughout the years. I have experienced seasons, sometimes lengthy, of feeling like the cloud of depression would not let up. My earliest memories of depression are of being an outgoing, extroverted teenager who had deep struggles with self-worth and self-image. I realize that all teens struggle with this, but it led me to medicate my loneliness with religion, girls, alcohol, or isolation. And none of those worked.

In my adult years, I have had intense battles with depression. Most would never know. I keep things going in work and life, but the internal battles are real. I remember going through the darkest time of our marriage, feeling like my chest was going to cave in. I was told by well-intentioned saints that I just needed to "trust God" and "know that He works all things together for my good." Romans 8:28 is a great verse but, when quoted at me, it seemed like a dismissal of my hurt and anguish. I felt like I was suffering alone.

When it comes to things like depression, most people suffer in silence. Individuals who are depressed feel weak and embarrassed. We get the sense that if we just "had it together" in our relationship with God, we would never feel depressed or have doubts. And nothing could be farther from the truth. Depression can often result from anger or hurt that gets turned inward. The anger gets suppressed or depressed. Basically, we bury our emotions and our hurts.

If you are hurting in your marriage and struggling to bury it, here are some words of instruction and encouragement for you today.

**WE MUST NOT SEGREGATE THE SPIRITUAL FROM THE EMOTIONAL.** God did not make a mistake when He gave us emotions. Like the dashboard on a car, your emotions are those "lights" that come on when something is happening under the hood (in your heart). Sure, our emotions can get us in a world of trouble. But, when channeled the right way, they can bring great freedom.

**DEPRESSION IS REAL FOR MEN AND WOMEN.** In some ways, our culture has misconstrued depression—assigning it to a certain gender or group of people. I want to validate both men and women who are struggling with depression. It is real, and our society is filled with people who feel empty and lonely.

**THERE ARE TIMES THAT DEPRESSION SETS IN DUE TO SIN OR HIDDEN ADDICTIONS.** There are also times that the stress and weight of life get a person down. Instead of viewing bouts with depression as spiritual weakness, it is much healthier to embrace the season you are in and see how God wants to father you in and through it.

**CONNECT ANGER AND DEPRESSION.** The connection of anger to depression is strong. Out of the setbacks, disappointments, and hurts of life, anger begins to surface. It is a normal reaction. We can spew it on others and hurt our relationships. We can bury our anger and suppress it, which equally hurts relationships. Many of our addictions, ways to medicate the pain and loss in marriage, are rooted in anger. We must find healthy ways to process and find healing with God for our anger.

**GOD OFTEN FATHERS THROUGH HARDSHIP AND ALLOWS DEPRESSION TO BREED DEPENDENCY.** At the core, God wants to father you as a son or daughter. Scriptures reveal God as Father. This is His heart and His character. He sometimes entrusts hardship or allows seasons of heartache for the purpose of dependency. He wants to tear down our man-made scaffolding and sufficiency and get us grounded in Him, which is what *humility* actually means. *Humility* comes from the Latin word *humilitas*, which means to be "grounded" or "from the earth." To be humble is to be dependent on God alone.

**YOUR NEWFOUND DEPENDENCY ON GOD COULD INFORM YOUR FUTURE MINISTRY TO OTHERS.** A husband or wife who has walked through the valley of depression, doubt, or fear is well attuned is well attuned to the rhythms of life and marriage. Journeying this road could grow you into a person who avoids quick fixes and formulas but instead offers a listening ear and a broad shoulder.

**JOURNAL YOUR EMOTIONS.** It is often hard for us to access our emotions. We simply don't always know what is happening under the hood. Journaling will help you to write out what is happening in your heart.

**EXPLORE THE PSALMS.** What a treasure we have in David's psalmbook. David understood that we cannot separate the spiritual from the emotional. Spend some time today in Psalm 143.

**GET HELP.** Lastly, I would encourage you not to fight alone. Every husband needs spiritual brothers, and every wife needs spiritual sisters. More than needing a mere accountability group, you need others who will listen and battle with you for restoration. If you are going through a dark season of depression, doubt, or fear, please reach out. Ask a friend out for coffee.

Seek out time with your pastor. Set up an appointment with a counselor. Do something to get help, and please do not walk through it alone.

## Reflections

- In what ways do you bury your anger or hurt?
- How do you feel depressed or sad about your marriage?
- Of the points listed in today's devotion, which one spoke the loudest to you?
- What phrase from Psalm 143 might be God's way of validating your hurt and speaking to your heart?

# YOU MUST
# DIG DEEP

*Therefore, since we are surrounded by such
a great cloud of witnesses, let us throw off everything
that hinders and the sin that so easily entangles.
And let us run with perseverance the race marked out
for us, fixing our eyes on Jesus, the pioneer
and perfecter of faith. For the joy set before him he
endured the cross, scorning its shame, and sat down
at the right hand of the throne of God. Consider him
who endured such opposition from sinners, so that you
will not grow weary and lose heart.*

—Hebrews 12:1–3

I (RANDY) have always been fascinated with Mt. Everest. From reading books to watching movies, there is something about this giant mountain that peaks my interest.

The most intriguing part of the climb is the final ascent. Some call it the summit push. As climbers near the peak of over 29,000 feet, much is asked of them physically and mentally. Most require the use of oxygen while climbing and the wear and tear on a person's body is debilitating. Some say that, at this stage, your body is actually dying from the lack of oxygen combined with fatigue. There is a window of time to reach the peak before descending the great tower in the sky.

I am sure that there is one phrase that could be applied to the summit push, "You must dig deep!" This is probably a phrase you need to hear today as you move through this season of marriage.

There are days when you want to give up. There are moments when it feels like too much. There are questions, fears, doubts, and confusion. And there is anger. Your anger may be toward yourself. How could I have done this? Why did I inflict such pain on my spouse? Why am I still in this marriage? Why did I not notice and act on the signs of distress in our relationship? Your anger may be toward your spouse or the situation. What was he or she thinking? How could these choices have been made? How has our marriage arrived at such a desperate place? Frustration . . . hurt . . . confusion . . . and anger.

The summit push in your marriage will require anger. That sounds weird, doesn't it? You might be thinking that merely love and forgiveness are required to restore your marriage. That is right. Forgiveness and change are vital parts of the healing process. Anger, though, is a necessary emotion to push you through the climb of restoration.

We tend to think of anger as a negative, almost god-less, emotion. We hear stories of how destructive anger can be in relationships. We hear of abuse and conflict that marks some marriages. Anger can be a destructive emotion when handled in unhealthy ways. If buried, it can lead to self-hatred and self-destructive patterns. If directed in unhealthy ways toward others, it can incite division.

Anger is an emotion, a neutral emotion. Although it can be destructive, it can also be used to fight for a marriage. The warrior heart in a man or woman that is needed to dig deep is fueled by healthy anger. Anger is deeply connected with passion and drive. When you want to quit, your anger can be used to keep you in the game. When you feel like throwing in the towel, your anger can fuel your next step of healing. When it feels like the marriage cannot withstand the elements of hurt and betrayal, your anger drives the process of forgiveness and restoration. And when the enemy, Satan, seems to be declaring a win in your relationship, your anger gives you the passion to fight and overcome the opposition.

We often refer to the last week of Jesus' life as the Passion. It is Jesus' final ascent, the summit push, leading Him to a hill called Golgotha or Mount Calvary. In the final hours of His life, oxygen levels are running low and fatigue has set in. The redemption of sinful mankind is at stake. Focused and digging deep, Jesus' heart is set on a mission. He will ascend this Cross, die a gruesome death, and achieve salvation for broken people. His passion was driven by anger toward sin and love to restore the broken relationship of His people with God the Father. His anger, though, was an expression of His love. At the peak of redemption, the words escaped His mouth, "It is finished" (John 19:30). Mission complete. And for those who believe, placing their faith on His broken, poured-out body, new life begins.

If you are going to dig deep in this season of marriage, it will not be through mustering up the energy or relying on your meager efforts. If you are going to fight forward, self-help or self-talk will be ineffective. Digging deep requires ruthless trust in the work and strength of Jesus Christ. It requires denying self and leaning on the power of God to do the impossible. And digging deep requires anger, anger toward the enemy, anger toward sin, anger toward giving up. Anger, as an expression of love, can be your driving force to trusting God for today.

## REFLECTIONS

⊚ How is physical or mental fatigue in your marriage affecting you today?

⊚ Describe the difference between unhealthy and healthy anger in a relationship.

⊚ How might your anger be used as a spiritual tool in your fight against Satan and in your fight for your marriage?

⊚ Hebrews 12 reminds us of Jesus' heart and mission of redemption. How can you display His heart today in your marriage?

# GREAT EXPECTATIONS

*Therefore if you have any encouragement from being
united with Christ, if any comfort from his love,
if any common sharing in the Spirit, if any tenderness
and compassion, then make my joy complete
by being like-minded, having the same love,
being one in spirit and of one mind. Do nothing out
of selfish ambition or vain conceit. Rather, in humility
value others above yourselves, not looking to your own
interests but each of you to the interests of the others.
In your relationships with one another, have the same
mindset as Christ Jesus: Who, being in very nature
God, did not consider equality with God something to
be used to his own advantage; rather, he made himself
nothing by taking the very nature of a servant,*

*being made in human likeness. And being found*
*in appearance as a man, he humbled himself by*
*becoming obedient to death—even death on a cross!*

---

ERRIAM-WEBSTER'S *Dictionary* defines *expectation* as the "belief that something will happen or is likely to happen." As I (Melody) read that definition, I already feel a twinge of angst over it. How many times have I had expectations in my marriage that went unfulfilled, and I was left feeling angry, resentful, and bitter? If I am honest, I have done it quite a bit. Expectations fill our minds all the time, usually without us being aware. And since our spouses are not mind readers, many of our expectations go unmet. We believe that something will happen. We assume that our spouse knows what we expect from them. (Granted, sometimes we have clearly expressed those things, but many times we have not.) Then, when our expectations go unmet, we are angry. We stew about it, yell about it, and harbor bitterness in our hearts. Sometimes we express it, but oftentimes we bury it. And it builds and builds until we blow up. It can be ugly. It can leave a person's heart wounded. It can have devastating effects on relationships that we value.

Randy and I spend a lot of time with couples, many who are in crisis situations. We've found that expectations are at the root of so many sources of conflict. Many of us were married believing that, given the right circumstances, our spouse would change in the ways we wanted him or her to. We believed that once we lived under one roof, things would be different. We thought family dynamics would be different. We thought addictions would go away. We hoped they would put us before their job, hobbies, parents, friends, etc. We believed we would be happier than we are. We thought having children together could make all things right. And the expectations put a burden on the marriage that it cannot withstand.

So, how do we function in relationships without letting expectations be the very things that drive us apart? I believe communicating the things we want and need is vital. We can get so busy doing life that we stop communicating basic needs to our spouses. The sad reality is that many couples go days and weeks without having any real, meaningful communication. If we quit communicating, we spend a lot more time assuming, and we end up angry that our spouses have not met our needs. I think a lot of couples struggling with heartache and broken relationships can trace the pain back to years of unmet expectations that were never clearly talked through.

I also believe it is never too late to start having those conversations. You may be at a point where you doubt your marriage can be saved, or the thought of saving it feels so overwhelming that you are not sure you have the strength to push through. Set aside time for conversation now. Talk about the places in your marriage where you have expected things from your spouse without clearly stating your needs. Own the fact that many of your expectations were too much for your spouse to fulfill in the first place. Don't accuse. Take ownership of the way that you have let your spouse down. If you approach your spouse with humility and a desire for healing, these conversations can break down walls of bitterness and resentment that time and hurt have built. If you approach your spouse with pride and anger, only further damage will be done. Ask God to give you a humble spirit and a willingness to extend and receive forgiveness.

Finally, it is vital to lay our expectations before the Lord. Many of the things we are expecting to be fulfilled in human relationship can only be fulfilled through our relationship with God. No human can meet all of our relational needs, build us up, keep us happy, or complete us. There is an emptiness placed in us by God for Him alone to fill. Take a close look at your expectations for your spouse, and pray for God to clearly show you where you are asking and wanting more than is healthy. Surrender your expectations to the Lord for Him to ultimately meet the desires of your heart. As you allow Him to fulfill you, you will find that the burden taken off of your spouse allows for healing and growth to begin.

## Reflections

⦿ How have expectations damaged your relationship with your spouse?

⦿ How do you believe you can better communicate your needs and desires to your spouse in humility and forgiveness?

⦿ How do Paul's words in Philippians encourage us to approach our spouses in a way that values them as individuals instead of valuing them based on what they can do for us?

# LONGING FOR JOY

*Consider it pure joy, my brothers and sisters, whenever you face trials of many kinds, because you know that the testing of your faith produces perseverance. Let perseverance finish its work so that you may be mature and complete, not lacking anything.*

—JAMES 1:2–4

D o you long to feel joy again? Do you feel like you would give anything for the weight of your pain to lift? Do you feel like you might never smile again? Even as I (Melody) type those words, I remember the feelings so strongly, and my heart feels heavy as I think back to the season in our marriage where I did not think I could ever feel anything but deep pain and sadness. I wanted to be hopeful that I might feel something good again, but it seemed impossible. I longed for joy.

So many Scriptures promise us joy. And even more encouraging, our circumstances do not dictate whether joy is possible. Honestly, it seems too good to be true. Joy in the midst of pain? Joy when we are not happy? Joy when life is falling apart? If Scripture is true, and I believe it is, then joy can be our reality, even when our hearts are broken.

Romans 15:13 is filled with great promise for us, "May the God of hope fill you with all joy and peace as you trust in him, so that you may overflow with hope by the power of the Holy Spirit."

Joy comes when our hearts are surrendered to Him. Does it make our pain, confusion, or anger disappear? No. But a heart that is surrendered to the sovereignty of God and trusts that He is at work in the midst of our anguish can experience joy, no matter our circumstances. Joy is rooted in trust. Trust brings us peace. And that means that joy is ultimately a choice. We choose to trust God. Our trust fills us with His peace. And our peace brings about a lightness of heart that is God's way of filling us with His joy. Joy gives us hope. Romans 15:13 can truly be a lifeline for us to hold onto when we are longing for joy.

Soak in these Scriptures today. Joy truly can be yours, through the power of the Holy Spirit at work in you during this time of marital hardship.

*You make known to me the path of life; you will fill me with joy in your presence, with eternal pleasures at your right hand.*
—PSALM 16:11

*When anxiety was great within me, your consolation brought me joy.*
—PSALM 94:19

*May the God of hope fill you with all joy and peace as you trust in him, so that you may overflow with hope by the power of the Holy Spirit.*
—ROMANS 15:13

*Rejoice always, pray continually, give thanks in all circumstances; for this is God's will for you in Christ Jesus.*
—1 THESSALONIANS 5:16–18

## REFLECTIONS

◉ Is your heart longing to feel joy? What fears do you have about surrendering your situation to the Lord?

◉ What steps can you take to release your situation to Him?

◉ Meditate on Romans 15:13 today. Ask God to help you trust Him, experience His peace, feel joy, and have hope.

# I'M TIRED
# OF TRYING

*Do you not know that in a race all the runners run,*
*but only one gets the prize? Run in such a way*
*as to get the prize. Everyone who competes*
*in the games goes into strict training.*
*They do it to get a crown that will not last,*
*but we do it to get a crown that will last forever.*

—1 CORINTHIANS 9:24–25

I F you've been married any length of time, you have thought and probably even said the words "I'm tired of trying." Relationship fatigue settles in as the fog of despair thickens.

Now, for the two people reading this who have never had such a thought or uttered such words: you are free to file this devotion away. But for the rest of us, the reality of wanting to throw in the towel is common ground. You are not alone in feeling that way.

The truth is, the relationship did not begin like this. Most relationships come out of the gate with lots of adventure, pursuit, intimacy, romance, and warm feelings. Think about the early days of dating and marriage. How did you meet? Where was your first date? When did you share your first kiss? Do you remember how you felt when you were together? While the early days of a relationship are not without disappointment, feelings of bliss dominate your time together.

The months or years pass by, and slowly you realize something is missing. Maybe an event takes place in your marriage that sparks mistrust or doubt. Or maybe your spouse, perched on a pedestal, comes toppling down after betraying you or disappointing you. And as the marriage hits the hard pavement of reality, your soul whispers, "I'm tired of trying. This is too hard. He or she will never change. This marriage will never be different than it is now. What's the use?" Just like walking out of a room and flipping the light switch off, darkness settles into the recesses of your heart.

This can be a dangerous place in marriage. It is the perfect storm for the enemy, Satan, to deliver subtle hints or direct temptations. In the vacancy of life and intimacy, someone or something can creep in and rekindle those desires for adventure, romance, and freedom. Affairs and addictions rarely show up as guests at the front door. They typically enter through side doors or hidden passageways. Aside from that, in the vacancy, despair can lead to a loss of heart and the choice to settle.

What do you do when you are tired of trying? Three thoughts:

ADMIT THAT YOU ARE TIRED OF TRYING. Our tendency is to think it and feel it without expressing it. We hide the feelings of relationship fatigue and try to maintain the image of "having it all together." We hold our cards and wait for our spouses to make the next move. Assumptions and unmet expectations need to be confronted with open, honest, heart-level conversation. Begin a conversation with your spouse, "I'm tired of trying . . . let me explain." Instead of blaming or using "you never" or "you always" statements, speak in first person, and share your frustrations.

FOCUS ON YOUR OWN FIELD. In Matthew 7:3–5, Jesus says,

> *Why do you look at the speck of sawdust in your brother's eye and pay no attention to the plank in your own eye? How can you say to your brother, "Let me take the speck out of your eye," when all the time there is a plank in your own eye? You hypocrite, first take the plank out of your own eye, and then you will see clearly to remove the speck from your brother's eye.*

Pointing fingers in a marriage is a way to direct our frustration outward. We get lured into the wrong battlefield of treating our spouse like the enemy. It is like looking out of your window, analyzing your neighbor's crops, and spewing condemnation their way. All the while, weeds creep into your own crops. Instead of peering out the window, we must look in the mirror and focus on our own field. Learn a deeper, truer walk with God in the midst of your despair.

EXCHANGE TRYING HARDER OR QUICK FIXES FOR A MIND-SET OF LONG-TERM HEALTH. Trying harder adds stress to a relationship by focusing on external changes. Attempts to merely change behaviors, fix your spouse, or develop superb communication skills are short-lived. Trying harder is like tinkering with the lights on your dash while the engine needs an overhaul. The engine of your life and marriage is your heart. And that is what Jesus came to ransom and redeem. Instead of merely trying harder, choose a process that yields long-term health. Be intentional about your walk with God, work through the pain, condition your soul, and stay in it. God delivers His strength in the midst of the process.

## REFLECTIONS

- In what areas of life do you currently feel like giving up?
- What temptations might the enemy, Satan, deliver in the midst of the desire to throw in the towel?
- Instead of merely trying harder, what are a few steps you could take that might bring long-term health to your marriage?

# THE VALLEY
# OF DESPAIR

*Therefore I am now going to allure her;
I will lead her into the wilderness and speak tenderly
to her. There I will give her back her vineyards,
and will make the Valley of Achor [trouble or despair]
a door of hope. There she will respond as in the days of
her youth, as in the day she came up out of Egypt.*

—HOSEA 2:14–15

HOSEA and Gomer had a model marriage in one sense of the phrase. It was not the idealistic marriage that you dream of. Gomer was a promiscuous woman; some believe she may have been a prostitute. Hosea was a servant of God, called to marry and be faithful to Gomer. Their marriage began with a faulty foundation of sexual sin and betrayal. It was not the model marriage. But, then again, it was.

Their marriage served as a model to the nation of Israel, and to us, of how God brings restoration in the midst of disaster. Their story highlights the faithfulness of God and our unfaithfulness. No matter your marriage circumstances, the truth is that we are all like Gomer. All of us have prostituted ourselves to the faulty gods of a broken world. And yet God, as faithful husband, pursues us and makes a way through the valley of despair.

The Hosea story played a key role in the restoration of our marriage. The morning after our marriage collapsed and following a restless night at a friend's house, I (Randy) decided to read my one-year Bible. To be honest, the last thing I wanted to do was read Scripture or talk with God. I was done. I was sad. I was angry. And God seemed distant at best. I had been reading the one-year Bible and decided I would turn to that day's reading. It was the December 5 reading—Hosea 1.

I tossed the Bible across the room in anger and said, "God, don't play games with me. I am not going to pursue this marriage." I knew the Hosea story and how God had worked through an extremely broken marriage. I knew that God was capable of doing the impossible. But my marriage seemed to be beyond all of this. And truth be known, my heart was beyond all of this.

Here are some loving truths from Hosea, particularly chapter 2, which will hopefully speak to you in your sadness and despair today.

## GOD BEGINS BY EXPOSING SIN.

In the early verses of Hosea 2, God seems cruel and harsh like a spouse who has been betrayed. His anger takes center stage as the betrayal and adultery of Israel/Gomer becomes clear. But isn't God's anger justified? Wouldn't a spouse's anger be justified? Of course. We must see anger in connection to love. God's wrath is a loving, honest response to betrayal and sin. The depth of anger matches the depth of love. God exposes Gomer's idolatrous ways and the betrayal in her heart. Israel is declared guilty as charged. The path of restoration in a marriage begins with honesty and ownership. Sin, wrongdoing, and mistakes must be owned by both spouses—acknowledging mutual brokenness in the relationship.

## GOD ALLOWS CONSEQUENCES AND DISCIPLINE.

Sin has consequences. After blocking "her path with thornbushes" (2:6), the consequences begin to unfold. From taking away grain, wool, and linen, to ruining vines and fig trees (2:9–12), punishment is now the return on sin. The temporary charm of sin eventually fades, and the effects set in. Part of the process of restoration is letting the consequences take place. One of the worst things we do in relationships is to delay or dismiss consequences in a person's life. Consequences are one of the primary ways that God loves and fathers us. God uses consequences to show us the broken state of our hearts, and to lead us in dependence on Him.

## GOD LEADS US INTO THE WILDERNESS.

Why would God allow or lead people into a wilderness time in marriage and life? I am sure that you are reading this devotion today because you are in some type of wilderness. Without the right perspective, wilderness times can be suffocating, confusing, and hopeless. But with the Hosea 2 perspective, we see the greater purpose behind the wilderness. The purpose of wilderness times, like the one you are in, is to bring you to a point of dependence on God. It strips us of our idolatry and sin, bringing us to the end of ourselves and to a point of surrender. It is at this point that God can bring restoration, healing, and hope. God desires for us to be redeemed and reconciled to Him. These wilderness times reveal the depths of His ways and His love for us.

## HE MAKES THE VALLEY OF DESPAIR A DOORWAY OF HOPE.

The whole Hosea/Gomer and God/Israel drama culminates in verse 15 when God says, "There I will give her back her vineyards, and will make the Valley of Achor [trouble or despair] a door of hope." And now the good news of restoration: redemption that comes in daily walking with God. All of this takes place so that God might do the impossible in our hearts and our marriages. Upon our surrender, God transforms the place of wilderness and despair into a place of freedom and hope. God's transformation of our hearts spills over into our marriages. Because He is at work to redeem us, He can certainly restore our marriages.

One last word: none of this happens easily or overnight. We wish this could happen in an instant and life be back to "normal." All of this is part of God's process of fathering His children and growing us in marriage. A husband and wife have to both be willing to surrender to God in the process of healing. Be encouraged today, and know that God is working in the valley of despair to bring hope.

## Reflections

- What stood out to you in the biblical story of Hosea and Gomer?

- What might God be trying to expose in your life for the sake of healing?

- What does it look like to surrender in the midst of the wilderness?

- Write Hosea 2:14–15 down, and carry it with you today. Be reminded of God's ability to restore broken people and broken marriages.

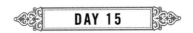

# I WANT TO RUN AWAY

*Where can I go from your Spirit?*
*Where can I flee from your presence?*
*If I go up to the heavens, you are there;*
*if I make my bed in the depths, you are there.*
*If I rise on the wings of the dawn,*
*if I settle on the far side of the sea,*
*even there your hand will guide me,*
*your right hand will hold me fast.*

—PSALM 139:7–10

Have you ever wanted to run away? I (Melody) remember being a child, and in moments where I felt my parents were being unfair, I would threaten to run away from home. I can even recall a time when my sister, at the age of seven or so, packed a bag and headed down our street because she was displeased with her Halloween costume. At the time I was worried that she would leave us forever. I am certain now that my parents found it to be a little comical; they knew she would not get far down the street before she realized she couldn't make it on her own and returned home.

I never envisioned that I would grow up and have some of those same feelings—wanting to run away. Adulthood has been much harder and more painful than I anticipated, and there have been many times when running away seemed easiest. Maybe you feel that way now. Your marriage is broken, you feel devastated, and the sadness in your heart feels like too much to bear. If you could run away from your life and have a reprieve, maybe you would survive it all. Is there a private island somewhere? Could you just hide in your closet? You desperately want a break from your sadness, and you don't know where to find it.

Since running away is not a healthy option for us, and it will not truly alleviate our pain, what can we do with those feelings instead? Rather than running away from our pain, we must run to God with it. For me, in a season of great despair over the possible loss of my marriage, I knew the only way to cope with the pain was to run to God. I had spent a great deal of time running away from God, which led me down a dark path of isolation. And when I was exposed in my sin, I knew that God was my only hope to become healthy and whole. I clung to Jesus in a way that I never had before. I had no Plan B. There was no escape. He was all I had, so I ran toward Him every day, praying for comfort and restoration.

Isaiah 61:1–3 (ESV) was a great help to me, and I believe it can be for you as well. These verses bring us such hope in our times of deepest sadness.

*The Spirit of the Lord GOD is upon me, because the LORD has anointed me to bring good news to the poor; he has sent me to bind up the brokenhearted, to proclaim liberty to the captives, and the opening of the prison to those who are bound; to proclaim the year of the LORD's favor, and the day of vengeance of our God; to comfort all who mourn; to grant to those who mourn in Zion—to give them a beautiful headdress instead of ashes, the oil of gladness instead of mourning, the garment of praise instead of a faint spirit; that they may be called oaks of righteousness, the planting of the LORD, that he may be glorified.*

What beautiful promises we receive! He binds up our broken hearts; He comforts those who mourn. He brings freedom to captives and gladness instead of despair. If we run toward God, rather than trying to run away from our pain and circumstances, His promises are rich and they are true. I am a living testimony that He will comfort and restore us when we cling to Him in our times of despair. Cling to Jesus. He is faithful.

## REFLECTIONS

◎ Do you feel like running away right now?

◎ Why is running away not the answer to our problems?

◎ What steps can you take today to run toward God? In prayer? In Scripture? With your time?

# GRIEVING
# TO HEAL

*I remember my affliction and my wandering,
the bitterness and the gall. I well remember them,
and my soul is downcast within me. Yet this I call to
mind and therefore I have hope: Because of the LORD's
great love we are not consumed, for his compassions
never fail. They are new every morning; great is your
faithfulness. I say to myself, "The LORD is my portion;
therefore I will wait for him."*

—LAMENTATIONS 3:19–24

WHEN dealing with an affair, an addiction, or a betrayal of trust in marriage, there are two tracks of grieving . . . two tracks of healing.

For the spouse who has been betrayed: you have been hurt on many deep levels. We want to validate the hurt, confusion, and sadness you are experiencing. You have unknowingly been following and believing a trail of lies. It is hard to know what to trust and hard to believe that you will ever trust again. Questions fill your mind:

*Was I not enough?*
*We had something good, didn't we?*
*Why was my spouse not honest with me?*
*How could my spouse do this to me and to us?*

You are now traveling a unique path. And this path is quite different from the one that your spouse will travel. First, we want to encourage you to grieve. The Book of Lamentations reminds us that grieving is a normal and necessary part of relationships. To love is to experience loss. To be vulnerable with another person is to risk being hurt. You know this quite well. Grieving and lamenting is our way of expressing what's inside of our hearts. And grieving is typically a mixture of sadness and anger. Those emotions can change moment by moment and day by day. If your marriage is in crisis, the emotions can be raw and volatile. If the hurt or loss in your marriage is in the past and was never grieved, the emotions might turn dull or numb. No matter where you are in the process, let yourself grieve.

Our second encouragement is to choose healing. Healing is a process, not a formula to follow. Your situation is unique and your loss is specific. Instead of trying to fix your emotions or your marriage, let your grief flow, and then choose to embark on a process of forgiveness and healing. There are important steps for your spouse to take. But, those are out of your control. Here's what you can control: you can choose to rely on God and to forgive your spouse. Be still and wait on God to heal and restore things. Let Him be your refuge and your portion in this unstable time.

If you were the one to betray your spouse, you probably feel like your sin and mistakes are on display. If things recently exploded, shame is surrounding you like a thick fog. Part of you wants to run away and medicate your pain with someone or something else. To run feels less painful than to stay. Part of you knows that you need to stay and see what God may want to do. Though the outcome is uncertain, you know that the only chance for healing is for you to stay put and work on your issues.

Your path is quite different from the one your spouse is traveling right now. He or she cannot fully understand what you are experiencing. First, we encourage you to grieve. To lament is to feel the weight of the wrong. To be broken, which is necessary for healing, takes place as we realize the ripple effect of our sin. This type of grief is painful and feels unending. The temptation to run will be great. The temptation to medicate your loneliness will loom large each day. Instead of running from God or your spouse, be honest in your grief. Even though you would love for this to pass quickly, something real and deep is taking place in the midst of the brokenness. Don't rush it and don't delay it.

We also encourage you to choose healing. Let the grief and weight of your sin push you toward a process of healing. Instead of letting this season overwhelm you, leading to self-hatred or shameful thoughts, commit to reconciliation. There are both spiritual and emotional reasons for the choices that you have made. Behavioral fixes might bring temporary relief, but they will not heal your heart. God wants to take you through a process that gets under the surface and heals the heartache that led to your sinful choices. Your heart matters, and God wants to do more than polish up the outside. He wants to heal your heart. Will you let Him?

The process of healing a hurting marriage involves two people choosing two paths that merge into one united story of healing. The paths are different based on the losses faced and the grief involved. The healing will be unique to your story and your loss. But if you both choose the appropriate path, God will do a great work of restoration in your marriage.

### Reflections

- Which path (of the two described above) best matches where you are?
- What is the hardest thing about being on that path?
- Where are you tempted to run or give up?
- How can grieving bring healing in your heart and potentially to your marriage?

# MY IDENTITY

*In all these things we are more than conquerors
through him who loved us. For I am sure that neither
death nor life, nor angels nor rulers, nor things present
nor things to come, nor powers, nor height nor depth,
nor anything else in all creation, will be able
to separate us from the love of God
in Christ Jesus our Lord.*

—Romans 8:37–39 ESV

**RELATIONSHIP TOXIN:** Believing the lies of the enemy about our identity

**RELATIONSHIP PRACTICE:** Believe that what God says about us is true

WHEN we walk through days of deep sadness, fear, anxiety, and uncertainty, Satan (our enemy) assaults our identity. He begins to speak lies about who we are, capitalizing on the pain of broken relationships, dashed dreams, and uncertain futures. If he can get us to question our identities, then he knows it will lead us to a place of despair—destroying our trust and hope in Christ.

In the darkest days of our marriage, I (Melody) felt like my identity had become equal to the circumstances of my marriage. Because I made choices that brought great brokenness to myself and to my relationships, it was hard to believe that I wasn't merely a label . . . broken, stupid, disappointing, hypocritical, or a failure. And that was just the beginning of the list. The lies of the enemy screamed loudly in my mind. It was a daily battle to fight against his efforts to convince me that I had ruined my life and marriage and that I would never be different.

The only way to overcome this onslaught of lies was to replace the lies with truth. In Christ, I was not just a label based on my sins and decisions. Because of Christ, and through His forgiveness, grace, and mercy, my identity was still rooted in Him. The blood of Christ had washed away the labels . . . but I must daily choose to align my mind to the truth of Scripture. I began to write Scriptures of truth about my identity on note cards, and place them strategically where I would see them throughout my day. I had to constantly remind myself that no matter what I had done, and no matter what the outcome of my marriage, that my identity was firmly rooted in the work of Jesus Christ.

Here are Scriptures that arm our minds for battle when we are in seasons of deep grief. We can live in victory over despair, even when our hearts are broken. I pray these are an encouragement to you today.

*There is therefore now no condemnation for those who are in Christ Jesus. For the law of the Spirit of life has set you free in Christ Jesus from the law of sin and death.*

—ROMANS 8:1–2 ESV

*He himself bore our sins in his body on the tree, that we might die to sin and live to righteousness. By his wounds you have been healed.*

—1 PETER 2:24 ESV

*I have been crucified with Christ. It is no longer I who live, but Christ who lives in me. And the life I now live in the flesh I live by faith in the Son of God, who loved me and gave himself for me.*

—GALATIANS 2:20 ESV

*Blessed be the God and Father of our Lord Jesus Christ, who has blessed us in Christ with every spiritual blessing in the heavenly places, even as he chose us in him before the foundation of the world, that we should be holy and blameless before him. In love he predestined us for adoption, as sons through Jesus Christ, according to the purpose of his will, to the praise of his glorious grace, with which he has blessed us in the Beloved. In him we have redemption through his blood, the forgiveness of our trespasses, according to the riches of his grace, which he lavished upon us, in all wisdom and insight making known to us the mystery of his will, according to his purpose, which he set forth in Christ as a plan for the fullness of time, to unite all things in him, things in heaven and things on earth.*

—EPHESIANS 1:3–10 ESV

## REFLECTIONS

⊙ What names and labels has the enemy placed on you during this time of difficulty and sadness?

⊙ According to these Scriptures, who does God say that you are in Him?

⊙ What are some practical steps you can take to let God's truth replace the lies in your mind and heart?

**DAY 18**

# THERE IS HOPE

*In you, L*ORD *my God, I put my trust. I trust in you; do not let me be put to shame, nor let my enemies triumph over me. No one who hopes in you will ever be put to shame, but shame will come on those who are treacherous without cause. Show me your ways, L*ORD, *teach me your paths. Guide me in your truth and teach me, for you are God my Savior, and my hope is in you all day long. Remember, L*ORD, *your great mercy and love, for they are from of old. Do not remember the sins of my youth and my rebellious ways; according to your love remember me, for you, L*ORD, *are good. Good and upright is the L*ORD; *therefore he instructs sinners in his ways. He guides the humble in what is right and teaches them his way.*

*All the ways of the LORD are loving and faithful
toward those who keep the demands of his covenant.
For the sake of your name, LORD, forgive my iniquity,
though it is great.*

—PSALM 25:1–11

W HEN your marriage has faced the pain of betrayal, loss, or disappointment, how do you find hope? How is it possible to have a stronger, more fulfilling marriage when you have faced such tragedy? We have been exactly where you are and know it is not easy. We now have a wonderful marriage, filled with love, trust, and a depth of intimacy we had never known before our marriage was broken. Getting to the place we are now has been a journey filled with many bumps in the road. There was no quick fix. It was a process. And we are still in process. We are thankful to know God will continue to heal and restore each of us individually and as a couple in the coming years. God is not done with us.

In the first few months after my (Melody's) affair was exposed, we both felt like a bomb had detonated. Our lives felt like a million shattered, scattered pieces, and putting everything back together again seemed impossible. But in those early days, God began to show us that He was not very interested in putting the pieces back together. He wanted to give us something new. Something healthy. Something strong. The old pieces represented faulty beliefs and flimsy scaffolding. We would never survive if we used those pieces to rebuild. He wanted us to start from scratch. So we did.

For a while, it felt like Randy and I tiptoed around each other. We each knew that the other was emotionally raw, and it was difficult to know how to relate. We were both so broken. We had no way of knowing if our marriage would ever be what either of us hoped for, but we knew that if we had a chance, it would only come through submitting ourselves to God and letting Him heal us.

We both had to choose to be broken before God and before each other. Our marriage had not gotten to such an unhealthy state without both of us contributing. I had to experience a heart of repentance for all of the harmful choices I had made over the previous two and a half years. We had to submit to God's work of refinement in our hearts and lives. It was painful. But it became our road to healing.

Days passed into weeks, and occasionally Randy and I would see a glimmer of hope. Things became a little less awkward. Trust started to return. We began to believe that we might survive. I prayed daily for God to restore love to our relationship. I longed for the day when I knew that Randy completely trusted me and I completely trusted myself. We knew we still had so far to go, but we were committed to the journey because we knew that God was committed to us. And that was enough.

As time passed, hope continued to grow. We learned to love each other with a depth that could only come from having lost our love. Joy found its place within our home. I began to see trust in Randy's eyes again. Life was not perfect. But we began to feel alive again. Our commitment to stay in our marriage deepened and went far beyond trying to do the right thing or protect our son. We wanted to be married to each other.

Randy has often said that our marriage may be marked by an affair, but it is not defined by it. We have faced some of the darkest days that a marriage can face, but those days do not represent the whole of our relationship. We will forever be changed because of what we have been through, but we stand in victory that God healed what was sick and restored what was lost. He has now given us a new marriage. Our relationship is still like every other marriage. We hurt each other's feelings, frustrate and disappoint each other, and drive each other crazy at times. But we also have a confidence that we are committed to each other for the rest of our days, and nothing can steal that from us.

## REFLECTIONS

- In times of sadness and fear, why is it hard to cling to hope?

- How do David's words in Psalm 25 bring comfort to your heart?

- In what ways do you need to surrender your heart to the Lord, in order for your hope to be restored?

DAY 19

# PARALYZED BY FEAR

*When the servant of the man of God got up and went
out early the next morning, an army with horses and
chariots had surrounded the city. "Oh no, my lord!
What shall we do?" the servant asked.
"Don't be afraid," the prophet answered.
"Those who are with us are more than those who are
with them." And Elisha prayed, "Open his eyes,
LORD, so that he may see." Then the LORD opened the
servant's eyes, and he looked and saw the hills full of
horses and chariots of fire all around Elisha.*

—2 KINGS 6:15–17

ELATIONSHIPS and stuckness go hand in hand. Feeling stuck is a normal part of marriage. But sometimes it can turn into paralysis.

Dan and Patricia just celebrated their two-year wedding anniversary and five years of being together. Over those years, they had become best friends and created memories through travel, home and pet ownership, church involvement, and shared activities. It was a near idyllic beginning. Dan worked in computer programming, and Patricia taught at a local elementary school. They had already made plans for future children and building a lifetime of memories together. The marriage, though, toppled off the idyllic pedestal a week after their two-year anniversary. Patricia discovered that Dan had an addiction to pornography. It was a struggle that had haunted Dan for years. Exposed to porn at an early age by a family member, Dan had tried to overcome the struggle with limited success. Patricia's world came toppling down along with hopes and dreams. Deep fear entered their marriage for the first time—paralyzing fear.

Reggie and Jamie got married 15 years ago and have three children. Life stays at a busy pace between jobs, kids, church activities, and hobbies. Most people at church would characterize them as the ideal or nearly perfect couple. They always seem to be doing a lot of great stuff for God and for others. On the surface, Reggie and Jamie are set for a great future together. But there are some underlying issues that have recently surfaced. Jamie has felt alone in the relationship for years. Reggie, a type-A personality, is driven and struggles to express emotions. He works hard at burying anger, sadness, and hurt because he fears hurting someone else. Jamie, on the other hand, feels things deeply and projects her emotions naturally. She can recall dozens of times that she tried to have deep, emotional conversations with Reggie while only getting a cold shoulder. Jamie has developed a friendship and emotional connection with someone at her local fitness center. Though seemingly innocent, she quickly realized that her feelings had crossed over into an emotional affair. When Reggie discovered messages between the two of them on social media, he was horrified and numb. For him, his worst fears for their marriage were being realized. For Jamie, the fear of being stuck matched her confusion over their future. Fear, crippling fear, clouded their relationship.

Bobby and Diana just celebrated 40 years of marriage. Their family commemorated the anniversary with a reunion of friends and acquaintances from the years. From gifts to shared memories and a photo album made by their children, the day marked a lifetime of relationships and marriage. Just after the reunion, Bobby retired from his job and joined Diana in creating their next chapter together. One day, he came in from the garage and found Diana staring out the kitchen window with the water running in the sink. "Diana, hey, are you OK?" Jolted by his question, she quickly went back to washing dishes and said, "Oh yes, sorry, I was looking at something outside." And Bobby went about his business of household projects. Truth be known, Diana was wrestling with fear—paralyzing fear. She wondered what the future held for retirement. Though their marriage of 40 years had been good, she felt a bit like roommates. She often tried to talk herself out of the fears but they lingered like a dark cloud. Wondering if the cloud would ever lift, she gazed back out the window.

Every marriage goes through seasons of stuckness accompanied by fear. Though it looks different for each of us, there are times when fear goes deep and becomes paralyzing. If you are there, you are in good company and there is a path forward.

Second Kings 6:8–23 features a great story about Elisha. He and his men were surrounded by the Arameans. During the night, Elisha's enemy encircled the city after receiving orders from their king to capture him. Early the next morning, Elisha's servant walked out to find their city engulfed by an army of horses and chariots. His response would be our response—paralyzing fear. In that moment, I am sure that an onslaught of questions, anxieties, and fears rushed through his mind and heart.

Elisha prayed. That's the first thing to do when fear knocks at your door. Then God opened his servant's eyes, and he looked up to the hills and saw horses and chariots of fire surrounding Elisha. God's army was encamped on the hills. Elisha's servant was consumed with thoughts of the enemy and impending doom. His fears surfaced from his circumstances. Elisha, though, reminds us to pray and look to God's army. Entrust your fears to God today and know that His power is greater than our fears.

## REFLECTIONS

⊙ Which of the marriages in today's devotion do you most connect with?

⊙ What fears do you currently have about your marriage?

⊙ How might those fears become paralyzing and debilitating for you?

⊙ What is God, through 2 Kings 6, reminding you to do with your fears today?

# SO MANY QUESTIONS

*Peace I leave with you; my peace I give you.*
*I do not give to you as the world gives. Do not let your*
*hearts be troubled and do not be afraid.*

—JOHN 14:27

S EASONS of heartbreak, sorrow, disappointment, and fear tend to be the times in our lives when our minds run rampant with questions. These questions can become crippling because they seemingly have no answers. Our minds swirl with fears, and then we begin to answer each question with the worst possible scenario. Hopelessness and despair can quickly set in, and we lose complete focus on the safety and sovereignty of God in our circumstances.

Have these questions crossed your mind during this season of marital difficulty?

*Will it always hurt this much?*
*Will we ever be happy again?*
*Can this marriage be saved?*
*Why did my spouse betray me?*
*Is this my fault?*
*Where are you, God?*
*Why did this happen?*

These questions are the first step in internally verbalizing our fears, and each unanswered question tends to lead to another. While pondering these questions is not a bad thing, what we do with them can lead us to a place of despair or lead us back to a loving God who wants to walk with us through our questions. Even though we may not get a direct answer from God immediately, His nearness to our hearts through our questioning deepens our relationship with Him in the midst of difficulty.

Learning to let go of our need to fix things, answer things, and know what is going to happen gives us the opportunity to lean on a Father who loves us deeply in our pain. He longs for us to depend fully on Him in the midst of uncertainty, and to trust that although we do not have the answers, He does, and will bring us the answers we need through Scripture, prayer, and the words of other believers. When we take these questions to Him, we find that He is a safe place and that even unanswered questions do not have to cripple us with fear.

Philippians 4:6–7 (ESV) is a passage that points us in a healthy direction with our questions.

> *Do not be anxious about anything, but in everything by prayer and supplication with thanksgiving let your requests be made known to God. And the peace of God, which surpasses all understanding, will guard your hearts and your minds in Christ Jesus.*

Verse 6 tells us that our questions belong with God. Through our conversations with Him, we can take the questions of our heart to Him. We do not have to chase them down roads that lead us to deeper anger, resentment, and fear. We can take the questions to Him. There is no question that He cannot handle and not one that He does not want to hear. Our questions are safe with Him.

Verse 7 follows with a promise that seems almost too good to be true. We are promised a peace greater than anything we can understand. And that peace will serve as a protection over our hearts and our minds through Christ. That is a promise we desperately need to believe and experience in times of pain and difficulty.

When the questions begin—and they will—we can either chase them down roads that will only make us more fearful, or we can surrender the questions to God. He will guard our minds with His peace if we are willing to surrender.

Sometimes in my own life, I (Melody) admit that I have wanted to hold onto the questions. I felt some strange sense of control if I let the questions roll around in my head in hopes that I could find the answer that I wanted. Surrendering the questions to Him brought a vulnerability that I was not sure I was willing to embrace. But, holding onto my questions only led to greater fear and insecurity. When I fully surrender my questions and their outcomes to Christ, peace is my companion. I encourage you today to surrender your questions to the only One who knows the answers and who longs to be close to you as you entrust your questions to Him.

## REFLECTIONS

◉ What questions constantly fill your mind? List them.

◉ Write a prayer of surrender. Entrust your questions to God, and embrace the gift of peace that comes with giving them to a loving and sovereign God.

**DAY 21**

# THE DARK CLOUD OF SHAME

*Instead of your shame you will receive a double portion, and instead of disgrace you will rejoice in your inheritance. And so you will inherit a double portion in your land, and everlasting joy will be yours.*

—Isaiah 61:7

I F you go to Google and type *definition of shame,* you'll see this result: a painful feeling of humiliation or distress caused by the consciousness of wrong or foolish behavior. What a great description of one of the most awful feelings we can experience. Shame: it covers us like a dark cloud, surrounding us with what feels like an inescapable power. We seek to avoid humiliation, but when our wrong or foolish choices bring humiliation into our lives or the lives of others, we long to crawl in a hole and hide. It can seem like shame hovers over us, whispering that nothing will ever be good again and pain will be our constant companion.

In my darkest moments, I (Melody) have felt like shame was a heavy coat that I was wearing, weighing me down and keeping me from believing I could hold my head up and look anyone in the eye. The weight of my shame led to feelings of hopelessness, fear, and despair.

But shame is a liar. Shame is one of Satan's most powerful tools to keep us stuck in our sin and despair. Shame causes us to isolate ourselves rather than seek help. Shame keeps us fearful—that others will always see us in a negative light, and our sin will be the truest thing about us. Shame tells us that we are marked by our circumstances, and we will carry that branding with us forever. Shame keeps us focused on ourselves rather than looking to Christ. Shame prevents us from hearing the truth of God's Word—the only pathway to our freedom.

Scripture tells us God does not shame His children. God sent Jesus Christ to not only cleanse us of our sins but to protect us from the grip of shame. God knows the power of shame, and His Word gives us multiple reminders that we are not to live under its shadow. The healing power of Jesus Christ's death and Resurrection have released us from shame, and we must daily choose to believe the truth over the lies.

First John 1:9 says, "If we confess our sins, he is faithful and just and will forgive us our sins and purify us from all unrighteousness." Our confession leads to our cleansing. When we come to Christ in humility over sinful choices we have made, then He promises to cleanse and purify us. Psalm 103:12 tells us, "As far as the east is from the west, so far has he removed our transgressions from us." He not only cleanses us but also removes those sins from us. They no longer have the ability to weigh us down and fill us with despair. Our confession and cleansing release us from the weight that shame brings.

Romans 8:1 gives us the glorious truth that those of us in Christ are no longer condemned: "Therefore, there is now no condemnation for those who are in Christ Jesus." If we are living under any condemnation, it stems from the enemy and ourselves, not from God. In Hebrews 8:12, God promises to extend bountiful mercy to us: "For I will be merciful toward their iniquities, and I will remember their sins no more" (ESV). God, in His unexplainable mercy, forgets our sin. That should bring us such freedom!

When we cling to these truths, shame loses its grip and power over us. Rather than believing we are failures, frauds, and forever tainted, we can believe the power of God's grace and mercy. He says we are forgiven, cleansed, no longer condemned, and that He has separated our sins from us through Christ's death on the Cross.

Friend, let us get out from under the dark cloud of shame. Let us confess our sins to God and embrace his mercy, grace, and forgiveness. We really can be free.

## REFLECTIONS

⊙ What kind of power has shame held in your life?

⊙ Has your experience with shame been like Melody's? Has it felt like a heavy coat that weighs you down and causes you to isolate yourself?

⊙ What can you do to make the truths of these Scriptures sink down deep into your heart so you can live from the truth rather than the lies of shame? Begin taking those steps today.

**DAY 22**

# OUT OF CONTROL

*Trust GOD from the bottom of your heart; don't try to
figure out everything on your own. Listen for GOD's
voice in everything you do, everywhere you go;
he's the one who will keep you on track.
Don't assume that you know it all. Run to GOD!*

—PROVERBS 3:5–7 THE MESSAGE

**RELATIONSHIP TOXIN:** Clinging to control

**RELATIONSHIP PRACTICE:** Releasing outcomes to God

WHEN you realize your marriage is in a place of brokenness, your lack of control becomes glaringly clear. Control—we all long for it. We work so hard to get control of ourselves, our people, and our circumstances. We believe that if we can just control our lives, then everything will turn out the way that we want it to and we can avoid pain, loss, and despair. The funny thing about control is, sometimes it appears to be working for us. People do what we want them to do. Things seem to be going our way. We feel like we've got it together. Whew! Being in charge of it all is working out just as we'd hoped!

And then our circumstances change, people change, and the illusion of control goes down the drain. We are not in control. Now all of the worst-case scenarios look like they may become a reality and despair can quickly set in. The cycle I (Melody) see so many of us living in, is one of fear, control, anger. Fear fuels our need for control. If we can just maintain control, the things we fear might not happen. So, we hold tightly to everything, grasping to keep everything in order. But, then something happens that reveals our lack of control, and we become angry. Angry that we can't keep all of the balls spinning, angry at the people who aren't falling into our plans, and angry that our circumstances are causing us deep pain. So, the fear deepens, we form new ways to control, the anger brews, and we continue the cycle.

Does this resonate with you? Have you tried to control your marriage? Has your spouse tried to control you? Has fear fueled your attempts to make everything work out the way you'd hoped, and now you realize that all of your attempts are failing? Is your lack of control over the future of your relationship paralyzing you? If so, you are not alone. Fear and control are common to us all. God is not surprised by our fears or our unhealthy ways of coping with them by trying to control our lives. Scripture is full of His directives. He commands us to not be afraid, but to replace that fear with trust in Him. Where we lack control, Jesus reminds us of the sovereignty of God. He is fully in control. Where we can't see what the future holds, He reminds us that He is holding our future. We must trust Him. We must release our need to control everything and rest in the assurance that He is at work in each circumstance we face. When we acknowledge that He is in control and trust Him to work all things out together for our good, we will experience His peace. We can release our need to control our outcomes and let Him do the work that He is already doing in and through us as we walk through painful times.

## REFLECTIONS

- How do we gain a false sense of power over our circumstances through control?

- Do you believe your desire to control your circumstances or the people in your life is the result of a deeply rooted fear?

- Do you feel angry when you are out of control?

- Can you take steps today through prayer and Scripture to release your need to control and trust God with the outcomes of your relationship?

# FATHERED

*But you, God, see the trouble of the afflicted;*
*you consider their grief and take it in hand.*
*The victims commit themselves to you;*
*you are the helper of the fatherless.*

—PSALM 10:14

OVER many years of counseling, we have noticed that one of the most important relationships in a person's life is the relationship with his or her father. A dad shapes a lot in his son's or daughter's life that shapes his or her image of God. In the Bible, God is revealed as Father (see Luke 15:11–32), and He has given us earthly fathers to help frame our understanding. For some, this framework is stable and a natural representation of God and healthy trust. For others, the framework is faulty, affecting our ability to trust God in the midst of fear or distress.

Fear affects all of us in marriage. At times, in hindsight we're able to understand that fear arises from shame, guilt, or remorse. In the present, our fears escalate as we consider our circumstances and the issues in our marriage. Looking forward, fear is fueled by the unknown and our uncertainty as to whether hope is even possible.

There is a vital connection between fear and being fathered. A person with a distant or hands-off relationship with God as Father will tend to be overwhelmed by fear and the unknown. A person with a close walk with God, who trusts Him as Father, is able to verbalize fear and declare faith in God.

What was your relationship with your father like? Here are some common fatherly archetypes we've seen in our years of counseling work and how they relate to fear (by all means, this list is not exhaustive).

**THE DISCONNECTED DAD**—I once heard a man say, "Dad was like a piece of furniture. He was physically there but emotionally absent." That's the disconnected dad. This father may pour himself into providing for the family but finds himself emotionally locked down. He may hide behind the television, a device, or a hobby. He is in the emotional "garage" tinkering around but removed from the family. A son or daughter is not allowed to share fears or any deep emotions that might be stirring within. A child is left to figure life out on his or her own.

**THE RICH UNCLE**—We have all heard of the rich uncle who sweeps into town and buys everyone's love through gifts and tangible representations of affection. Once or twice a year, after little contact or communication, he abruptly pays a visit and takes center stage. And just after unwrapping gifts or enjoying a nice meal, his car pulls out of town, leaving everyone with a look of disbelief. If your parents divorced or dad had a job with travel, you might connect with this one. When a father behaves like a rich uncle, a son or daughter is left asking, "What just happened?" He or she has no time to deal with fear because of the limited communication. Eventually, a child's dreams of a close relationship fade into the sunset of a lost relationship.

**THE GOD WITH A BIG STICK**—Maybe you grew up in a family where dad was the primary disciplinarian. Almost militant, dad was the one who kept everyone in line and enforced behavioral rules. Or maybe you grew up in a religious environment that placed rules over relationships. In a legalistic culture like that, good behavior trumps an honest and open heart. Either way, a child is left with constant fear. *Dad basically only comes around when I mess up.* So, what are you left to do with your fear? Bury it so that no one knows. This kind of relationship fuels a subsequent life of denial and dishonesty.

**THE ABSENT FATHER**—Once, I met with a woman who recounted her parents' divorce when she was in elementary school. From what she remembered, mom and dad simply could not get along and eventually got divorced. Standing in the driveway with dad pulling off, she said, "I waved good-bye never realizing that he was literally driving out of my life. He was gone—absent." What a tragedy! Some respond by hiding and running from fears into their adult years. Others respond by becoming driven and compensating for fears with success. Either way, their fear is pushed aside or buried.

**THE WELL-MEANING GRANDFATHER ON THE PORCH**—Some dads just want their kids to be happy without providing any form of discipline. This leads to imbalance in the relationship and fosters mistrust over time. Though it brings temporary happiness, a person is left without the necessary boundaries for life. Fear cannot be entrusted to this type of father because he would never understand or be able to help.

**THE ALCOHOLIC DAD**—Growing up with an alcoholic or addicted father leads to a guessing game. A child never knows what kind of father he or she will encounter in the home. In the absence of stability and sometimes in the presence of abuse, a child hides or acts out to get attention. A culture of fear is created where family members feel unsafe or on their own.

**GOD**—He is the Father who loves, protects, and pursues. The Bible reveals God as a loving Father. Jesus, being God in flesh, came to reveal the Father's heart and character. Jesus said, "Anyone who has seen me has seen the Father" (John 14:9). The Holy Spirit is God's fathering presence with adopted sons and daughters on a daily basis. God loves and protects those who belong to Him. He pursues us even when we are running away. And God welcomes us to bring our fears, doubts, and hurts to Him. He will not turn a blind eye or dismiss our fears. There is no guessing game with God. He is deeply connected to our lives and is willing to grow us through any trial or hardship.

Trust God today with your fears. Let Him father you. No matter what your relationship has been with your earthly father, lean on God and find rest in being fathered by Him.

## REFLECTIONS

- Which of the father examples above do you most connect with?

- What are the first five words that come to mind when you think of your dad?

- Growing up, what did you learn to do with your fears?

- God is offering to father you today. Be honest with Him about your fears, and declare bold trust though the way you live.

# FROM FEAR
# TO FAITH

*My God, my God, why have you forsaken me?*
*Why are you so far from saving me, so far from my*
*cries of anguish? My God, I cry out by day, but you*
*do not answer, by night, but I find no rest. . . . I will*
*declare your name to my people; in the assembly I will*
*praise you. You who fear the* LORD, *praise him! All you*
*descendants of Jacob, honor him! Revere him, all you*
*descendants of Israel! For he has not despised or scorned*
*the suffering of the afflicted one; he has not hidden his*
*face from him but has listened to his cry for help.*

—PSALM 22:1–2, 22–24

T HE prison cell was beginning to feel like a bottom-less pit. And that was a familiar place for Joseph. Joseph had taken the brunt of other people's choices for a long time. Thirteen years before, his brothers, wishing him dead, threw him into a pit, and sold him into slavery. Potiphar's wife, jealous and vengeful, pushed him through a set of lies into the prison that was now his home. Forgotten by a cellmate who made empty promises, Joseph has waited for two long years (see Genesis 37; 39–41).

Can you imagine the fear that must have crept into Joseph's cell and into his heart? Feeling forgotten manufactures great fear. Sometimes, we feel forgotten in a marriage. Whether you are newly married or a seasoned veteran, you might know the feeling of being "left behind." You have probably felt like your needs were overlooked or dismissed at different times. And the marriage that was once blissful has turned into a prison of sorts.

*Prison* sounds like a strong word, doesn't it? The truth is, fear can put us in a real prison.

**PAST-TENSE PRISON OF FEAR**—In looking back at your life or at your marriage, you might be filled with some regrets. You may even question whether you married the right person. If you have made some bad decisions, as we all have, you have remorse. Fear becomes a prison when we let our past define us. Instead of trusting in God's ability to redeem broken people and broken circumstances, we focus on old wounds and wallow in old choices. It is a prison, indeed.

**PRESENT-TENSE PRISON OF FEAR**—Looking at your marriage right now, you probably have a lot of questions. Fear takes our questions and turns them into statements. *Will he or she ever forgive?* becomes *He or she will never forgive.* *Can this marriage be restored?* becomes *This marriage will not be restored.* *Can I trust again?* becomes *I will not trust again.* Fear, when fueled by Satan, can put a final period where God may want to place a comma. Faith in God does not overlook or dismiss our fears, but instead it rises above them and declares trust in the God who does the impossible. God can do far more than your fears let you believe.

**FUTURE-TENSE PRISON OF FEAR**—In thinking forward, you might wonder if marriage will ever get better. *Can we move beyond this season? Will we get over this? Can we fall back in love again? Are there better days ahead of us?* Fear, when placed in the future, becomes fueled by the unknown. And to be honest, we like to be in the know. You may be tempted to say, "I will only work on this marriage if I know that my spouse is going to do the hard work, too." Who are you putting your faith in? Your efforts? Your spouse's efforts? Or in God's ability to work through a process? Faith declares that God has the future and that my role is to relentlessly trust Him even when I don't feel like it or necessarily see God at work.

We know from Joseph's story in the Book of Genesis that God did a work of restoration in his life. But, we must not overlook the years of waiting and potential fears that he must have experienced. Tossed into a pit, Joseph had to declare faith in the midst of his fears. Forsaken by his own family, he had to trust in God's goodness and plan. Arrested and placed in prison, Joseph had to walk close with God to keep fear from taking over. His life is not an exception or a story of super-human strength. Joseph's life is just like your life. A different set of circumstances with a different set of fears. But the one thread running through all of our stories is that God is trustworthy. Choose faith in the midst of your fear today.

# IN THE
# WILDERNESS

*The LORD is my shepherd; I shall not want.*
*He makes me lie down in green pastures. He leads me*
*beside still waters. He restores my soul. He leads me in*
*paths of righteousness for his name's sake. Even though*
*I walk through the valley of the shadow of death,*
*I will fear no evil, for you are with me; your rod and*
*your staff, they comfort me. You prepare a table before*
*me in the presence of my enemies; you anoint my head*
*with oil; my cup overflows. Surely goodness and mercy*
*shall follow me all the days of my life, and I shall*
*dwell in the house of the LORD forever.*

—PSALM 23 ESV

WHEN walking through seasons of heartbreak and pain in your marriage, life can feel very much like a wilderness experience. As if we are the only ones who have felt pain the way that we feel it, and there is underlying loneliness that can permeate all of life. The wilderness feels vast, and we feel small in it.

But God has given us a beautiful passage in Psalm 23 to remind us that in our wilderness times, which feel like valleys in the shadow of death, He is with us. For many of us, Psalm 23 is such a familiar passage that we miss the richness of its message. We can find rest for our weary souls in its words.

In verses one through three, God, our Shepherd, reminds us that He has provided everything we need. He insists that we rest, leading us into places of beauty to bring awareness of His presence and restoration for our hearts. He assures us that even in our loneliness, we are not alone. He will guide our steps when we are willing to let Him lead us through the darkness.

Verse four uses imagery comparing us to sheep, dependent upon Him for everything. Even when we walk through valleys that feel like death, we do not have to be afraid of what will happen because He promises to be with us. When your marriage is broken, it can feel like a death. It is the death of hopes, dreams, and a relationship as you thought it would be. The enemy, Satan, wants to use this season of your life for harm or destruction, but God says we do not have to be afraid of evil. He is present with us in our brokenness. His rod and staff can comfort us because they are the ways that He can draw us close to Him—to bring us protection and peace in the midst of loss and pain. We are safe in Him.

Psalm 23 closes with a beautiful picture of coming to the table where we are esteemed by the hands of God. He meets our physical and spiritual needs and anoints us as His beloved sons and daughters. We can reflect on how He has carried us through dark times in the past and find peace in the knowledge that He goes before us as we take the next steps toward finding greater wholeness in Him. When we entrust our lives to Him, we can find rest in His grace and mercy through every season of wilderness.

## REFLECTIONS

- Do you feel like you are in a wilderness right now, filled with loneliness and fear? If so, what is one step that you can take to trust God in the wilderness?

- Does the difficulty in your marriage feel like a death? If so, in what ways?

- If Psalm 23 is familiar to you, was there anything in the passage that stood out to you in a fresh way given your present circumstances?

# I CAN'T FORGIVE

*Be kind to one another, tenderhearted,*
*forgiving one another, as God in Christ forgave you.*
*Therefore be imitators of God, as beloved children.*
*And walk in love, as Christ loved us and gave himself*
*up for us, a fragrant offering and sacrifice to God.*

—Ephesians 4:32–5:2 ESV

Tᴍᴇ seemed to stand still as I (Randy) sat in the parking lot of a rest area. Our marriage had collapsed a week earlier and, on this day, things had begun to sink in. The fog was clearing from the initial few days of shock, and now the reality of a new normal was staring me in the face.

I left our house a few hours before and decided to take a drive—a long drive. With no destination in mind, I remember getting on the interstate and heading out. To some extent, I was running away. I wanted a break from the thoughts, doubts, fears, and anxiety. But I quickly discovered that the fears and hurt were along for the ride. In other ways, I was running toward something or someone. Lonely and confused, I wanted someone to step in and fix all of this. But our relationship seemed beyond repair.

After a few hours of silence on the road, I saw the rest area sign and took the exit. It was late at night, and the parking lot was pretty empty. I pulled into a spot and immediately began to weep. There is crying, and then there is uncontrollable weeping. This was the latter of the two. I felt so alone, lost, and filled with fears. So many questions poured through my mind about life, our marriage, and the unknowns of the future. And in this quiet moment, I began to hear the whispers of forgiveness. God was not demanding or dictating that I forgive. He was inviting me to consider the process of forgiveness. To be honest, I had to forgive Melody, and I had to forgive myself. I blamed myself for much of what we were going through.

In the parking space at the rest area, the words sprinted from my heart to my lips, "I can't forgive!" It felt like too much of a burden. Forgiveness seemed like an island miles away. I could see it, but there was no way to get there. How could I forgive

Melody for the wrong in our marriage? How could I forgive myself for neglecting her needs and allowing our marriage to fall apart? How could I overcome the self-hatred and self-blame that filled my life? How could I get over the loss? And could our marriage ever be restored?

Forgiveness is a tough thing in relationships, isn't it? Every relationship needs it, and every person struggles to give it. To be in relationship is to risk being hurt. In fact, you will be hurt. You can spend your life running from the pain, attempting to escape grief, or you can walk through it and be shaped by it. There is a direct correlation between grief and forgiveness. To grieve something is to say it mattered and it hurt. To grieve is to admit the loss. And grief ultimately opens our hearts to forgiveness, Godlike forgiveness. For God so loved the world . . . and felt the weight of sin . . . that He gave His Son . . . that He gave forgiveness.

A few thoughts on forgiveness for today:

FEEL THE WEIGHT OF THE WRONG. Instead of living in denial or downplaying the pain, let yourself feel the loss. Grieve it. If you tend to hide your tears or hurt, give yourself permission to be angry and sad. Whether you were the person who betrayed trust or the one betrayed, you must feel the weight of the wrong. It is hard. It is emotionally fatiguing, but the process of forgiveness begins with brokenness and grief.

LET YOURSELF GRIEVE. How do you handle grief? How do you typically express emotions such as sadness or anger? If you are a processor, then your tendency will be to hide your grief. Buried inside, these emotions can lead to depression, self-hatred, or bitterness. You must find ways to talk about and get your feelings out on the table. Choosing to hide your emotions prevents grief and healing. Let yourself grieve. While some of us are processors, others of us tend to wear our emotions on our sleeves. You tend to feel things quickly and respond quickly. Your grief needs time. Don't feel like you have to rush through this or make quick decisions. Let yourself grieve.

EMBRACE THE PROCESS OF FORGIVENESS. Forgiveness is not like a light switch that can quickly be turned on or off. It is definitely a process. But the process must begin with a choice. Out of the forgiveness that you have been given in Jesus Christ, ask God to give you strength in weakness and the ability to embrace the process of forgiveness.

I finally pulled out from the parking lot at the rest area. My eyes were still blurry from crying, but there was a new resolve in my heart. Though I felt like I could not forgive, I made a decision that night to take the next step toward restoration. I began to drive back home, uncertain about the future, but certain about what God had spoken. Who would have ever thought that a rest area could literally be a *rest* area?

## REFLECTIONS

⊚ What first comes into your mind when you think of forgiveness?

⊚ What do you need to own, confess, and ask forgiveness for today?

⊚ Who do you need to forgive today?

⊚ How might God's forgiveness of you give you the ability to embrace a process of forgiveness?

# EVERY MARRIAGE NEEDS A DIVORCE

*When he came to his senses, he said, "How many of my father's hired servants have food to spare, and here I am starving to death! I will set out and go back to my father and say to him: Father, I have sinned against heaven and against you. I am no longer worthy to be called your son; make me like one of your hired servants." So he got up and went to his father. But while he was still a long way off, his father saw him and was filled with compassion for him; he ran to his son, threw his arms around him and kissed him.*

—LUKE 15:17–20

T HE title of this devotion may be confusing or intriguing. Yes, we are proposing that divorce is needed in your marriage—but a divorce of a different sort. Not the type of divorce that involves lawyers and settlements and finality. Not the type of divorce that leaves a person to figure out life on his or her own. The divorce that we are recommending is very different. It comes from the truth of Scripture being realized in our own marriage and walk with God.

Married in 1995, by December of 2003, we were facing divorce—an actual, legal divorce. We were at the point of seeking the advice of lawyers and figuring out how to share custody of our child, drafting financial agreements, etc. We thought it was our only choice.

Then, we discovered a new definition for *divorce*. We entered a process that allowed us to divorce the former marriage and life without ever getting a legal divorce. We were able to start over in a new relationship with the same person. Would it have been easier to divorce and start over with another person in another marriage? Not really, because this divorce forced us to deal with things we would have taken into another relationship. How rewarding to be able to deal with things in our own lives while maintaining a marriage that would benefit from our personal efforts. The rich history we built over the years would not be lost—only enhanced. We would now have a fuller story of walking through a divorce while being married.

When we speak of divorce, in this context, we are actually referring to biblical brokenness and repentance. Divorce/repentance paves the way for restoration with God and with your spouse. That is why we like to say that every marriage needs a divorce because every marriage needs repentance.

Based on the story of the loving father and the two sons in Luke 15, we find that there are two types of marriages.

**THE LEGALISTIC MARRIAGE**—The older brother in Luke's account represents a legalistic marriage. Lacking in repentance, this marriage is defined by measuring and trying to keep score. Spouses look at each other and try to stay one step ahead. Performance becomes the measuring stick for how the marriage is doing. If you want to check the temperature of this relationship, just look at how much is being accomplished. You can even use religious activity to justify the health of the relationship.

This produces isolation and hiding in the marriage. Because there is no freedom to be honest about failures and flaws, the marriage declines into communication only about the "good stuff." Anything that tastes of struggle cannot be shared. A basic hypocrisy surfaces, and the marriage becomes stale and lifeless.

Steve struggled with pornography. He hid it from his wife, Lydia, for many years, until one day it was discovered. Lydia found some things on his computer that alarmed her and led to confrontation. Lydia's words pierced his heart when she said, "If you ever do this again, we are done. You disgust me, and I will not spend my life with someone like you."

So Steve doubled his efforts and started down a path of fixing his problem. It worked great for several weeks, even months. Lydia asked a few times, and he was able to respond with, "I'm doing great, you don't have to worry about this anymore." That worked for a while. Eventually, it did not come up much and things seemed OK. The marriage was fine, or was it?

The lustful lure returned for Steve, and he found himself steeped in pornography once again. He knew that he could never tell Lydia or anyone else. It would destroy her and their marriage. He remembered her words so vividly, "If you ever . . . I will . . ." He knew exactly where that was headed. So, he hid. He kept it all secret. There was even some self-justifying talk going on, "Certainly, God does not want my marriage to fall apart. If I share this, I will lose my family and mark my children's lives forever. So, I will just handle this myself."

What do you think happened to Steve and Lydia? On the outside, things seemed OK. They continued to function as a family, raising children and planning their future. But, there was this slow deterioration of their relationship. In the Gospels, Jesus talked about the "yeast of the Pharisees." Yeast is a small living organism that gets added to dough. In fact, it's added in such a small amount that you cannot see it. But over time, while simmering and multiplying in the lump of dough, it causes the dough to rise. Just a pinch of yeast affects the entire loaf.

This is the danger of legalism in a marriage. It is minute and small. In fact, it is often imperceptible from the outside. But when it seeps into a relationship, the outcome can be deadly. The marriage may stay intact, but it will die a slow death. Lacking honest repentance, a marriage will decline into behavior management and score keeping. Without true repentance, performance stifles love and grace. But there is another path available.

**THE REPENTANT MARRIAGE**—The second type of marriage is represented by the younger son in Luke 15. We find him coming to his senses, owning his sin, and choosing to walk back home to his father.

Steve and Lydia could have chosen this path. They may not have even known it was available. You may not even know this is available. While the legalistic marriage leads to death and ultimately suffocates love, the repentant marriage has life written all over it. It is the kind of relationship that reflects God's grace and unconditional love. It is a marriage that breeds freedom.

Now, let us be quick to point out that the repentant marriage is not light on sin and does not excuse failure. It takes sin seriously. Repentance is always preceded by honest ownership of sin and deep brokenness. As we have said, brokenness paves the way for healing. Repentance is basically taking ownership of your own journey, struggles, and failures. It looks sin in the mirror and does not turn its back. Instead, it sees—really sees. While denial dismisses repentance, transparency welcomes it. It always begins with honest ownership of your own stuff. Instead of looking to fix your spouse and work on their stuff, repentance is a personal journey that leads you to look at yourself before evaluating others.

Let's return to the story of Steve and Lydia. Go back to the scene where Steve was found out. Caught in sin and a lengthy struggle, how could this have turned out differently? First and foremost, the sin would not have been dismissed. It would have been seen for what it is—loss of relationship. In a legalistic structure, sin is viewed as missing the mark or a behavior glitch. But in a repentant environment, sin is taken much more seriously. It is viewed as the loss of life and relationship. Choosing to sin is much more about choosing death over life. So, Steve and Lydia would have been broken over the sin in their marriage.

Contemplating Steve's struggle with pornography would have led them to a season of grieving and despair. No doubt, Lydia would have experienced confusion, hurt, anger, and betrayal. Her husband, friend, and lover had been grasping for life in other places. This, in turn, affected their relationship and formed holes in their intimacy. Relationship was broken and trust misplaced.

At this point in the repentant marriage, Steve and Lydia would have been honest about their feelings and entered into a process. What a keyword for the repentant marriage: *process*. Not formula. Not a fix-it plan. Not denial or condemnation. But a process. This is a vital mind-set for a marriage committed to healing and restoration. It only comes by entering into a process that sees sin for what it is and seeks to usher in healing through Jesus Christ.

We have seen many couples walk through dark times where the finger gets pointed at the "sinner," the spouse who committed adultery, had the struggle, or made a fatal mistake. While that spouse has caused a lot of heartache and pain, the repentant marriage does not point fingers but extends a hand. A hand that says, "Let's walk through this together." And so a process begins.

REFLECTIONS

◎In your own words, describe the difference between a legalistic and a repentant marriage.

◎How can you fight for a repentant marriage?

◎What is one step that you can take today toward restoring hope in your marriage?

# ULTIMATUMS
# AND BOUNDARIES

*See, I set before you today life and prosperity,
death and destruction. For I command you today
to love the LORD your God, to walk in obedience to
him, and to keep his commands, decrees and laws;
then you will live and increase, and the LORD your God
will bless you in the land you are entering to possess.
But if your heart turns away and you are
not obedient, and if you are drawn away to bow down
to other gods and worship them, I declare to you this
day that you will certainly be destroyed. You will not
live long in the land you are crossing the Jordan to
enter and possess. This day I call the heavens and the
earth as witnesses against you that I have set before you*

*life and death, blessings and curses. Now choose life, so that you and your children may live and that you may love the L*ORD *your God, listen to his voice, and hold fast to him. For the L*ORD *is your life, and he will give you many years in the land he swore to give to your fathers, Abraham, Isaac and Jacob.*

—DEUTERONOMY 30:15–20

WHEN you begin to question the future of your marriage, or doubt that you have a future at all, your heart can lead you to a lot of dark places. Fueled by hurt, disappointment, and anger, we say and do things that we never believed we were capable of. We think if we gain control over our situation and our spouse, then maybe the pain will ease a bit. And we begin to throw out ultimatums in order to gain some sense of security. Ultimatums are always driven by our fears. Ultimatums use threats to get our spouse to do what we want them to do. And maybe if our spouse complies, we feel like we have the result we were looking for. At least temporarily.

But ultimatums come at a high price—the price of choice. If we begin to throw out ultimatums to gain control or security, we ultimately strip away the opportunity for our spouse to choose us, to choose the marriage, to choose healing. A marriage salvaged by fear-driven ultimatums cannot heal. Any marriage that is broken can only experience healing and restoration if both spouses are given the choice to stay or the choice to walk away. None of us wants to be with a spouse who is only with us out of fear and obligation. To know that your spouse has chosen you and your marriage brings greater security than any fear-driven ultimatum ever could.

When we quit giving ultimatums, and instead use healthy boundaries to protect us, we may begin to see a glimmer of hope that we did not know was there.

We oftentimes confuse boundaries and ultimatums; we think we are setting boundaries when we are really giving ultimatums. Boundaries define healthy and acceptable behavior and provide an opportunity for someone to choose to live within those parameters. When a marriage has been wounded, betrayed, or broken, healthy boundaries allow us to rebuild trust. Boundaries provide safe places to begin to develop new ways of relating. Unlike ultimatums, which are meant to evoke fear in our spouse, boundaries offer safe lines to fall into and give the other person the choice to live within those boundaries or not. No threats, no force, just an invitation to choose something different.

I (Randy) believe one of the reasons our marriage went from being deeply broken to the beginning stages of being healed is that we never gave each other ultimatums. It would have been easy for each of us to make a list of things that had to happen—or else. But by God's grace, we didn't do that. However, we set clear boundaries and a clear understanding that living within those boundaries was necessary in order for our relationship to have any possibility of restoration. Were the boundaries hard? Yes. Were they helpful? Yes. And they gave both of us the opportunity to choose the marriage, not out of fear of what might happen if we didn't comply but out of freedom because it was what we desired to do.

Healthy boundaries are biblical. Scripture is filled with places where boundaries were given for the protection of God's people. From the beginning of time, God has set boundaries for us to live within, but He desires for us to choose Him. He does not use fear and ultimatums to get people to believe in Him, live for Him, or walk in relationship with Him because relationships ruled by fear are not relationships at all. Instead, God gives us boundaries and choice. A relationship that is chosen is the only kind of relationship there really is.

## REFLECTIONS

- Has your marriage been marked by boundaries or ultimatums? Have you thought about this before?

- Do you believe setting healthy boundaries might provide an opportunity for your marriage to experience healing?

- What boundaries do you believe need to be in place for trust to be rebuilt?

# I SEE
# GREEN GRASS

*May the God of hope fill you
with all joy and peace in believing,
so that by the power of the Holy Spirit
you may abound in hope.*

—ROMANS 15:13 ESV

**RELATIONSHIP TOXIN:** The grass is always greener on the other side.

**RELATIONSHIP PRACTICE:** Stay focused on my own grass

W E'VE all heard the phrase "the grass is always greener on the other side," and I (Melody) believe there comes a point in most marriages where we start to wonder if that statement has merit. We begin to compare our marriage to other relationships we see, and suddenly our relationship seems to fall very short. Or we come to the realization that everything we believed our marriage would be at this point has not come to fruition, and the disappointment leads us to believe there must be something better out there. The grass we're standing in begins to appear brown and dull, and the grass around us looks a bright shade of green. "Don't I deserve better?" we begin to ask. "Why can't I have a relationship like theirs?" or "Why isn't my spouse the man/woman I thought I married?" and "Doesn't God want me to be happy?" The questions begin to roll through our heads, and suddenly we're convinced that, ultimately, what we deserve must be elsewhere.

There was a time in our marriage when I saw grass that I believed was much greener than the grass of my own marriage. I thought I deserved a different level of happiness than what I was experiencing, and I was giving up hope that things could or would change. I was disappointed, frustrated, and relationally immature. Rather than seek wise counsel, share my thoughts and feelings with a trusted believer, and be completely honest with Randy, I chose to believe the lies of the enemy. His whispers became loud, and my unhealthy heart began to listen and believe that the lies were truth. The grass looked greener outside of my marriage, and I let a friendship become an affair. I believed that God had held out on me, let me marry the wrong person, and that the plan of my life was all wrong. God had messed it up. I had messed it up. I no longer saw my life through the right lens.

I believed the lie that the grass must be greener in a different relationship. A relationship that was based on a false reality. I quit looking at my own grass. My marriage was not hopeless, and it was not beyond growth or repair. It had lost its focus and center on Christ. Had I been more willing to surrender my own plans, desires, and expectations to Christ, I would have made very different choices. No person is meant to complete us, fulfill us, or meet our every need. And oftentimes that is the weight that we place on our spouses. We want them to fill every empty place within us. The truth is, only Christ can fulfill us and fill those places. The only green grass we are ever promised is in the safe, protective life that we have in Him. We cannot look to another person to fulfill the role that only Jesus can.

The beautiful reality of God's redemptive plan is that He can restore the relationships that we believe are beyond hope.

## REFLECTIONS

- In what ways have you believed that the grass is greener outside of your marriage?
- What are the longings of your heart that are unfulfilled?
- How can you begin to surrender those longings and depend on Christ to fill those empty places in your heart?
- Will you trust God to bring restoration to your heart and marriage today?

# A NEW CHAPTER

*For this reason I bow my knees before the Father, from whom every family in heaven and on earth is named, that according to the riches of his glory he may grant you to be strengthened with power through his Spirit in your inner being, so that Christ may dwell in your hearts through faith—that you, being rooted and grounded in love, may have strength to comprehend with all the saints what is the breadth and length and height and depth, and to know the love of Christ that surpasses knowledge, that you may be filled with all the fullness of God. Now to him who is able to do far more abundantly than all that we ask or think, according to the power at work within us, to him be glory in the church and in Christ Jesus throughout all generations, forever and ever. Amen.*

—Ephesians 3:14–21 ESV

I HAVE had enough. I am done," exclaimed Elijah as he sat down under the shade of a tree. It had been a long journey, and he was ready to check out.

Just a few days before, Elijah had experienced miracles as he called down fire from heaven against the prophets of Baal (1 Kings 18). These false prophets had questioned God and questioned Elijah. With God's reputation at stake, Elijah fought and overcame the enemies in remarkable fashion. But now Elijah faced a new enemy.

Her name was Jezebel, and her power surpassed that of the Baal prophets. She was relentless in her anger and ruthless in her pursuit of Elijah. "Mark my word," she said, "Your life belongs to me, and I will destroy you." And so Elijah ran for his life. Arriving in the wilderness, exhausted from the journey, he collapsed under a tree to get a break and hide out. Fatigue had set in, and Elijah was done, finished. There was no more fight in him: his life did not even seem worth living (1 Kings 19).

Maybe you can connect with Elijah's plight. Maybe you have memories of overcoming great enemies, but the one you are staring at now feels like too much. Maybe your marriage has overcome some obstacles over the years, but the one you're experiencing now feels like a giant, brick wall. It is hard to imagine a new chapter when you are emotionally and physically spent. Throwing in the towel might seem like the only viable option with everything that has transpired in the relationship.

What happens when exhaustion sets in? Elijah took a nap. He fell asleep under the shade of the tree. While Elijah was asleep, God delivered some food through the culinary creativity of an angel. It truly was heavenly cuisine. He ate and then slept some more. A second time, the angel called him to get up and journey forward. The journey eventually took him into another wilderness: a cave on the side of a mountain.

The loneliness of the cave provided another opportunity for God to speak to him. On a side note, it seems that wilderness times tend to be where God does his best work. When we reach the end of ourselves God begins His work. God's strength shines forward in our weakness. It was in this cave conversation that God asked Elijah the question, "What are you doing here?" It was as if God was saying, "Elijah, I know you have had enough and that you are done. I know you have given up. But I am not done. I have not given up. I'm writing a new chapter in your story." God spoke in the loneliness and silence of the cave.

And then God gave some interesting instruction, "Go back the way you came" (1 Kings 19:15). The way forward was to actually go back. The next chapter in Elijah's life hinged on retracing his steps. Sometimes God does a work of healing in our lives by taking us back. He will surface things that have been hidden or denied in order to bring restoration. And He does the same thing for a marriage. For a new chapter to be written in your marriage, it may require going back. You may have to revisit places where you have hurt your spouse and ask for forgiveness. You may need to unearth some wounds in order to extend forgiveness to your spouse. It is in going back, experiencing brokenness and healing, that we are able to move forward with life and marriage. No matter what your spouse does, you have a choice to remain paralyzed in the present or move forward by going back.

Out of this wilderness context, Elijah was called to retrace his steps. In doing so, the next chapter of his life could be written. God had another assignment for him that involved anointing and appointing some new leaders. One of those would become his successor, Elisha. A new chapter in Elijah's life came after a season of despair and hopelessness.

We are not here to paint a pretty picture about restoration in a marriage. And we are not here to make empty promises about the outcome of your relationship. There are many unknowns about your particular situation and hopelessness. But we do want to declare that God is able to write a new chapter. God allows and sometimes orchestrates seasons of wilderness in order to speak and do something new. He ushers in brokenness for the purpose of healing and restoration. This work must begin in you and overflow into your marriage. Are you ready for a new chapter?

## REFLECTIONS

- In your own words, describe the feeling of being done or having had enough.
- Describe this wilderness season in your life and/or in your marriage.
- How is God calling you to retrace your steps and go back in order to go forward? Where are the places that forgiveness needs to be received or offered?
- Do you trust that God can write a new chapter in your story and marriage?

# A STORY TOOL

O NE of the foundational components to our counseling approach is story. We spend several sessions working through a man or woman's family diagram in order to identify themes that have shaped a person's understanding of God, marriage, trust, sexuality, self, etc. Three words frame our understanding of our story and reflect the gospel/Jesus story in our lives. *Beginnings* point to the early years of a person's life and/or marriage. It is important to go back and detail some of the early influences in your life. It is also helpful to remember the early years of marriage. *Brokenness* enters a person's story through crisis or the loss of innocence. Marriages tend to come in and out of seasons of brokenness. This second movement in a person's story or a marriage story involves the entrance of sin, mistakes, hurt, and loss. *Restoration* is the final movement in story that sets relationships back in order and recovers hope.

The three elements of story (beginnings, brokenness, and restoration) are a mere reflection of the truest story . . . the gospel story. God, who had no beginning or end, created a beginning in Genesis 1 and 2. Brokenness quickly entered the story in Genesis 3 with the presence of Satan and human sin. God breaks into the human story through the life and work of Jesus Christ, His perfect Son. Restoration takes place for those who entrust their broken hearts and broken lives to Him. The restorative power of Christ continues in a believer's life through the presence of the Holy Spirit. This is God's way of fathering us, loving us, and guiding us on a daily basis.

Take some time to work through your story and/or your marriage story. Here are some questions to guide your journey.

## BEGINNINGS
1. First, take some time to retrace your own steps. Find the best way to organize your early years. Maybe you could categorize the

years by homes you lived in, schools you attended, key events, etc. Once you have a handle on that, think through the key elements of each period of time. Who were the important people in your life? What did you learn about trust, expectations, love, acceptance, God, marriage, family, etc.? Did you incur any emotional or spiritual wounds during these years?

2. Describe each of your parents. What were they like and how was their marriage? What did you gain from those relationships? What did you lose from those relationships?

3. Your marriage also has a beginning. Reflect on the early years of your marriage. What were they like? What are some fond memories or experiences you shared together? How did you meet? What was your first date? First home you lived in? It is great for a couple to spend time reflecting on the early years of marriage.

## BROKENNESS

1. As a child, what were some of the broken scenes in your story? When do you remember feeling like innocence was lost, like something was stolen? Some examples could be parents' divorce, abrupt loss or death, a relocation/move, relationship struggles, sexual exploration, abuse of any sort, etc.

2. A word that most couples can connect with is *stuck*. Most of us have faced times when we have felt stuck in the relationship. Things don't always turn out the way we think they will. When have you felt stuck in your marriage?

3. Many marriages have times when their stories get messy. You may or may not have experienced a season like Melody and Randy shared. But you can probably connect with feeling lost,

confused, or desperate at some point in your marriage. When have you experienced that over the course of your marriage?

4. Where are you currently struggling and feeling stuck in your relationship? Maybe a financial fog, a communication breakdown, a career dead end, parenting confusion, etc. Share some of your current struggles.

## RESTORATION
1. How has God redeemed and restored some of the broken scenes in your story? How has He used the tragic seasons of your life to shape you and grow you?

2. How has God redeemed and restored some of the broken scenes in your marriage? How has this helped you grow in relationship with God and your spouse? Maybe you long to see God redeem those broken places in your marriage. Put words to that also.

3. Give an example of a time when God used someone's story to inspire you toward a deeper walk with God.

4. How might sharing your story of restoration help you overcome the enemy and claim victory in Christ?

5. How can sharing your story of restoration help others or give them hope?

# LOVING YOUR HUSBAND

Wives, we want to encourage you in the journey of loving your husband. Here are some helpful reminders.

1. LET GOD FATHER YOU—First and foremost, a woman needs to bring her identity and brokenness to God. Let Him father you, bringing you the love and validation you need. A husband was not meant to complete you but to complement you.

2. KNOW YOUR HUSBAND'S STORY—Do you know about his early years? His childhood adventures? What about his relationship with his dad? How did his dad show love and affection? Did he receive validation from his dad? Did he hear the words, "I love you" and "I am proud of you"? And what about his mother? Was she merciful or controlling? What did she show him about relating to a woman? And what was their marriage like? What about his relationships with women prior to you? What about his wounds, hurts, and struggles in being a man?

3. KNOW HIS CORE FEARS—Men are afraid of failing. Whether career, finances, relationships, or simply mowing the yard, a husband doesn't want to mess it up and fail you, fail God, or fail others. As a woman, this helps you understand the lens through which a man sees life and makes decisions. Do you know his core fears?

4. RESPECT AND TRUST—Men feel loved when they feel trusted. Though a woman cannot validate a man, she carries a primary role in providing affirmation. A man will often feel disrespected when treated like a boy or mothered. To try to tame a man or control him is to say, "I don't trust you." Obviously, some men have lost trust through bad decisions and the trust must be rebuilt.

5. NEED HIM WITHOUT BEING NEEDY OF HIM—Both sides of that phrase are important. This frees him up to grow as a man without all the pressure. Give him space to be a man. When he wants some adventure, time alone, let him go. A man needs places in his life where he has room to be a man. Most men find their hours filled in a cubicle or office, grinding at the job, meeting deadlines, and trying to muster up a living. This can suffocate a man's heart. A woman loves a man when she

says, "Go," and doesn't keep score. (Here, we're not referring to seasons of difficulty. Needs ebb and flow. When a spouse is experiencing illness or depression, he or she may need more affection and care. This a general principle for everyday life, but, of course there are some exceptions here.)

6. SUBMISSION VERSUS VULNERABILITY—Submission, found in Ephesians 5, is a command given to husbands and wives. Submit to one another. But there is a unique way that a wife submits to a husband. To submit is to choose to be vulnerable. One of the greatest gifts a woman gives to her man is her vulnerability. To be vulnerable is to entrust your heart to him. And that's really what he wants.

7. CHALLENGE HIM PRIVATELY—But yes, do challenge him. Be strong and confident enough as a woman to challenge something in him. But be wise in choosing the right setting, and never challenge him in front of your children.

8. SEXUALLY . . . HOW DOES A MAN WANT TO BE LOVED?—It is such a gift for Eve to offer her beauty to her man. He wants your heart, your vulnerability, your strength, and your beauty. This is true in the context of sex in marriage. To offer your body is to offer your beauty. If there is sexual brokenness in your past or in your marriage, enter a process of spiritual and emotional healing. Seek out counsel from a pastor or a professional counselor.

9. BE A STUDENT OF HIS MASCULINE HEART—Take some time to read and study how a man walks with God. If you have sons, that's an added incentive for doing this. A man's core desires, fears, and brokenness are uniquely different from a woman's. God meant something when He created man. Know and be familiar with the masculine journey.

When asked, "When do you feel loved?" here are some responses from husbands:

*Chase after dreams with me.*

*Feeling appreciated for going the extra mile and providing for the family.*

*Respected, valued, and appreciated.*

*Know my heart and my dreams.*

*Allow me to be a leader.*

*Light up when she sees me.*

*Encouragement, affirmation, smiles, and laughter.*

*Understand that I can't flip a switch and be "emotionally on."*

*Physical touch—nonsexual and sexual.*

*Pray for me and trust me.*

*Respect my ideas and opinions.*

*Don't expect me to read your mind.*

*Openly discuss life together.*

*Intimate sex on a regular basis goes a long way.*

*When I am her focus, not her job and not social media.*

*To know she thinks about me, even when we are not together.*

*Affirmation that I'm a good husband and father.*

*Please don't mother me. I'm not another child in the home.*

*Present a united front to the kids, discuss disagreements behind closed doors.*

*Affection.*

*Understand the weight I carry, of providing for the needs of our family.*

*I want to be her knight in shining armor.*

*I want her to be proud of me.*

*Know that I am trying really hard. Extend grace and forgiveness.*

*I want her to desire me.*

*Initiate time with me.*

*Be my true partner through thick and thin.*

*Encourage—don't attack or accuse.*

*Relax some and don't feel like you always have to accomplish something.*

*Love me enough to allow/encourage me to pursue some manly adventures.*

# LOVING YOUR WIFE

H USBANDS, we want to encourage you in the journey of loving your wife. Here are some helpful reminders.

1. VALIDATION—This is foundational. Because of the brokenness of man stemming from the fall in Genesis 3, a man looks to Eve for validation. A woman can easily become man's source of worth and value. When given the power to validate, a wife is equally given the power to devalue. Woman cannot validate man. This is something only God can provide for a man. You must look to God to father you, validate you, heal you, and empower you.

2. KNOW HER STORY—To fight for and shepherd a woman's heart, a man must know her story. How much of her story do you know? Do you know the intricacies of her early years? What hurts and wounds does she carry? What is her relationship with her Dad like? And Mom? What about her dreams and desires? There is no formula for loving a woman. Spend time getting to know her story, not just the facts but also what lies beneath the facts.

3. FIGHT FOR HER—There is a battle taking place, which means that she has an enemy. Satan has a target on the heart of your woman. She bears God's image in her beauty, strength, vulnerability, and mercy. And the villain hates her for it. Instead of fighting her, you must battle with her against the enemy. Based on her story, what are the specific ways that she has been opposed: comparison, self-image, wounds, doubts, fears, etc.

4. SHEPHERD HER—If the battle calls forth the warrior, then shepherding calls forth the lover/shepherd in a man. Every woman carries wounds, hurts, and struggles. As trust is earned, a man is able to extend the mercies of God toward her wounded, sometimes fearful heart. God alone can heal and strengthen her, but you can pave the way for that to happen.

5. ROMANCE HER—In the dating phase, a man pursues and

romances. He goes out of his way to make her feel special. Once married, there is a tendency for romance to be replaced with work, paying bills, raising children, and completing household projects. Romance, though sometimes spontaneous, is most often a choice. Plan date nights. Plan a weekend getaway. Surprise her with a favorite gift or treat. To know that you are thinking of her will do wonders for her heart.

6. TALK TO HER—Most men are doers more than talkers. Men want a task to complete or a project to manage. But a woman's heart cannot be treated like a project or to-do list. Talking involves both listening and sharing. Listen to her without distractions or an agenda. Look her in the eyes when she is talking. Instead of shutting down, share about your day, your frustrations, and your hopes. Model honesty and transparency in the marriage.

7. KNOW HER CORE FEARS—Insecurity, fear, and anxiety are lifelong companions for a woman. Some women compensate through drivenness and control while others retreat and hide relationally. What are you wife's core fears? How does she feel "not enough" in your marriage? How does she feel like "too much" in your marriage? Fear can be a ploy of Satan to defeat your wife and diminish her faith in God. Know her fears and commit to walk with her to overcome them.

8. BECOME THE SPIRITUAL LEADER OF YOUR HOME—Most men hear that statement and feel overwhelmed. To be a spiritual leader sounds like achieving supersaint status. Nothing could be farther from the truth. A spiritual leader is the chief servant in the home. He thinks about others before himself. He models brokenness and honesty. He admits his wrongs. And he encourages family members to trust God. Do not think of spiritual leadership as perfection or sainthood. Think of it as living a life of honesty, dependence on God, and humility.

When asked, "When do you feel loved," here are some responses from wives:

*I want to be known.*

*Instead of fixing me, I'd rather have a listening ear.*

*I want to feel special.*

*I need to "see" your love.*

*Defend me and take up for me.*

*Be interested in my past —thoughts, dreams, doubts, and fears.*

*Keep your word. Follow through on what you said you would do.*

*A loud and abrasive tone shuts me down.*

*Pursue me in nonsexual ways.*

*Know my passions and my goals for life.*

*I want you to be the first to say, "Let's pray about that."*

*Verbal praise makes me feel loved.*

*Simple affection in public, like holding hands or putting your arm around me.*

*If I don't feel like you know or care for me, I am not going to open up sexually.*

*Romance me and flirt with me.*

*I love dates, especially when he handles the details.*

*Small gifts, particularly on "non-holidays."*

*Initiate spiritual conversations.*

*I want you to be a warrior and a lover.*

*I want to fight against the enemy with you, so include me in your prayers and Bible study.*

*I want to feel treasured.*

*Communication is very important to me.*

*I want to matter to you.*

*Help me experience alone time—time just for me.*

*Let's talk about our walks with God.*

*Lead our family toward a deeper walk with God.*

*I want to feel special and loved deeply.*

*Pray for me, and let me know that you are.*

*I want to feel secure and stable in our relationship.*

New Hope® Publishers is a division of WMU®, an international organization that challenges Christian believers to understand and be radically involved in God's mission. For more information about WMU, go to wmu.com. More information about New Hope books may be found at NewHopePublishers.com New Hope books may be purchased at your local bookstore.

Please go to
**NewHopePublishers.com**
for more helpful information about
*30 Days of Hope for Hurting Marriages.*

If you've been blessed by this book,
we would like to hear your story.
The publisher and author welcome your comments and
suggestions at: newhopereader@wmu.org.